Hieronymus Bosch

Sandra Orienti - René de Solier

HIERONYMUS BOSCH

D.R. BOOKS
London

CONTENTS

Illustrations

Introduction

We know comparatively little about Hieronymus Bosch, one of the most disturbing and problematic painters of the fifteenth century in Europe. As early as 1604 Karel van Mander admitted to knowing nothing about him, and only recently has historical research enabled us to reconstruct a few basic data, although there are still many gaps. Such data have to be read and understood in the context of the complex world—mental and imaginative, religious and social—in which the artist lived.

Bosch was of provincial stock, and outwardly remained provincial. He was born in northern Brabant, in the city famous for its flourishing trade and industry and its markets in textiles, pins and knives, known as Bois-le-Duc in French, and in Dutch as 's-Hertogenbosch. He took his name from the last syllable of his birthplace, and was called Hieronymus Bosch.

In reality his surname was van Aken (or Aeken, or Aquen, or Acken), indicating that his family came from Aachen.

His date of birth has been fixed by general agreement around 1450; his date of death in 1516 can be seen in the records of the Brotherhood of Our Lady, to which the painter belonged insignis pictor *(as a distinguished painter), according to the brief entry.*

Other facts and references, though sporadic, can also be gleaned from the records of the Brotherhood (Lieve-Vrouwe Broederschap) to which "Jheronimus Anthonissoen van Aken" (i.e. Hieronymus son of Anthony van Aken) was admitted in 1486.

Two years later, in 1488, having become a "notable", he took part in the Banquet of the Swan, to which the painting of The Marriage at Cana *undoubtedly refers. In July of the same year he welcomed his fellow-members to his house which stood in the market-place of the town.*

He is also mentioned in the Brotherhood's books for the years 1488, 1492, 1503, 1508, 1512, and finally, as we have said, for the year of his death.

But a little more information is available besides this: around 1478 Bosch married a rich burgher's daughter, Aleyt van de Meervenne (born in 1453), who brought him as her dowry a house and some land at Oirschot, about thirty kilometres from 's-Hertogenbosch, to which the painter probably retired from time to time to work.

In 1480–81 Hieronymous supplied—and he is described as a painter in the documents—two panels of a triptych which his father Anthonius had left unfinished. He belonged, in fact, to a family of painters; it was the profession not only of his father, but also of two uncles and his grandfather, Jan van Aken, who died in 1456, leaving in the Cathedral a Christ Crucified dated 1444.

In 1493–94 Bosch drew the cartoons for the stained glass windows in the Brotherhood's chapel in St John's Cathedral, a chapel for which he had also painted some Biblical scenes which were lost when it was sacked by the Protestants in 1629.

In 1505 the painter was commissioned to paint three escutcheons, and in the following year he received an advance of 36 florins from Philip the Handsome for a painting which was to show the Last Judgment with Heaven and Hell; perhaps the Vienna Last Judgment, or the Munich one, which has come down to us in a fragmentary state.

In 1508–9 the Priors of the Brotherhood of Our Lady asked advice from Bosch and the architect of their chapel, Jan Heynste (or Heyns), on the colouring and gilding of a carved altarpiece, engaging them to check the finished work. In the same year the Brotherhood discussed a modest payment to the painter, who had produced a design for a copper candelabra.

In 1511–12 there are other reports of work with the Brotherhood; there were no other painters on their rolls, so that they turned to Bosch even for minor tasks: the master designed a cross, or crucifix, perhaps intended as part of the Brotherhood's vestments.

Finally, there is the report of his funeral.

But there are other facts and circumstances that can help us to reach the essence of Bosch's work, and to decipher, at least partly, the complex and disturbing symbolism of his paintings. These consist of details and incidental events which, when related to the historical, religious and social climate of Brabant, the region of the Netherland where the painter lived and worked, shed light on the meaning of his work.

Alaert du Hameel, architect, was in charge of work on the Cathedral of St John at 's-Hertogenbosch from 1478 to 1494. He completed the south aisle of the transept and laid out the central nave, showing off to the full the grotesques adorning the arches of the choir, which, together with other Gothic and Late Gothic sculptures and ornaments, must certainly have been a source for Bosch's fantastic elaborations.

But the relationship between the painter and the architect may have gone further. Not only were they close friends; Alaert's qualifications were those of "mason, master of the Lodge, stone-carver", besides that of engraver in copper, by which he became the interpreter of Bosch's work. And in the context of research into the function and importance of the architect and the first lodges, a few interesting details can already be found in The Marriage at Cana, where Bosch not only seems to be portraying the kind of banquet a Lodge might have had, but also builds the composition around a table in the shape of the letter L. In the same picture, among the dishes carried by the serving-men, there is one with a swan, the symbol of the Brotherhood of Our Lady, and the allusion to initiation rites is obvious in the emphasis laid on the presence of various objects.

These hints are already enough to call up for us a singular world, and, within it, Bosch's strange, immense culture, depending above all on his knowledge of sciences and disciplines that are hermetic, forbidden or "accursed", from astrology to Judaic teachings, from alchemy to demonology, from Gnosticism to apocalyptic allegories. This vast knowledge shows when the works are analysed. For example, the lives of hermits in the desert and their temptations is a constantly recurring theme in Bosch's work—and here we see how he interprets the relationship between mysticism, and food and drink in the light of information given in accounts of the saints' lives; these accounts describe the mystical practices used by saints and hermits to make themselves receptive to revelations about the self and the world. But then the whole of the popular and learned tradition of the period in which the painter worked is fused together in his art: passages from the Bible and the Apocalypse; the Golden Legend; the De Divinatione Daemonum of St Augustine; the life and work of the mystics who prepared the ground for the persecution of heretics, persecution which was later to become a furious struggle against witches and sorcery; and, first among these mystics, the "doctor admirabilis", Jan Ruysbroeck (The Spiritual Tabernacle, The Shining Stone, The Four Temptations etc.) and the writings of Albertus Magnus (the De Animalibus, for instance) and of Denis de Rijckel; the revelations of the Dominican Alain de la Roche (Alanus Redivivus); the Malleus Maleficarum of Jakob Sprenger, a sort of detailed manual for inquisitors and the enemies of heresy, published in 1484, the same year in which Innocent VIII issued the Papal Bull Summis Desiderantes Affectibus; The Ship of Fools of Sebastian Brandt, published in 1494; the Bestiaries; the Visio Tundali, first published in Antwerp (1472) and then in 's-Hertogenbosch itself, in 1484; the sombre Ars Moriendi and all the hagiographies and martyrologies, proverbs and mystery plays; and with them all the even more popular folk material, the superstitions and survivals of ancient myths and beliefs, the public tortures and hangings, the terrifying sermons and the obsession with fear, the processions and masquerades.

All these are sources, and others, more detailed, could be added; even if they are not strictly relative to the formation and constructions of Bosch's peculiar language, they are still linked with the inventive store of images, the latent purposes concealed in the imaginative elaboration of symbols and their meanings, sometimes glowingly obvious, sometimes elusive, complex, ambiguous, not so much because the painter desires it so, but rather because we lack the key, which always relates to the exacting, acute and spasmodic psychology of Bosch and his times.

There is an ample bibliography which also helps us with this interpretative side of Bosch's painting and the value of the sources and references: Franz Cumont with The Egypt of the Astrologers; Baltrusaitis who, in Le Moyen Age Fantastique, made it possible to interpret some of Bosch's strange and entirely individual figures, the "grilli" or freaks; René Guénon, for the study of traditions, and Henri Corbin who, through research on the philosophy of Islam, introduces other new elements into the mediaeval Christian tradition of the West. Regarding the relationships between food and mystical practice, the function of plants and fungi and the inherent power of visionary suggestion, it is only right to mention the researches of George Dumézil, Gordon Wasson and Roher Heim, and, relating more to the history of religions, those of Mircea Eliade.

The reprinting of the works of Fulconelli (1928) has been of fundamental value for the study of alchemy—which is one of the principal sources through which we can discover the key to Bosch's work—as are also the essays of Eugène Canseliet (L'Alchimie et le Mutus Liber).

The writings of Lacan (1966) relate a large part of the problems of Bosch to Freudian doctrines, especially with regard to the Lisbon Temptations, recalling Tolnay's remarks (1937) about the functions of psychoanalysis in relation to the same painting.

Still with regard to this work and those thematically related to it, and the complex witches' sabbath that it shows, we have to refer to the studies of Enrico Castelli and the Annals of the Congress on Humanism and the Demoniacal in Art (1953) which include fundamental contributions by A. Chastel, W. Fraenger, P. Francastel, H. Sedlmayr, L. Baldass, and, in addition, to other works including those of R. Villeneuve (Erotologie de Satan, 1962) and P. Richer (Etudes sur la grande hystérie, 1885).

Reference can be made to the Bibliography for the rest of the copious literature on the subject, not specialising in the individual problems of Bosch's work so much as surveying the artist as a complex totality into which the problems of painting and of his peculiar language are grafted and fused in a profusion of symbolic meanings and moralistic and ideological aims.

Chapter I

BOSCH AND HIS TIMES

In the autumn of the Middle Ages, the night was darkening, shot with warring flames and flickering, obsessive visions.

The world of Bosch's imagination was crowded with symbols, swelling with meanings; he collected and reflected, pinning down every shape as if beneath a lens—the terrors and desires, the agonies and hopes of his noisy, satanic world, menaced by thoughts of sin, temptation, judgement and hell.

Flashes of light and flames of fire illuminate the convulsed and twisted humanity of his paintings; often there seem to be transient gleams of pure light, but in the insidious contrasts with the deep shadows they give a sharp cutting edge to the picture. The connection of meanings and symbols seems then to be irrefutable, bound to the chain of a logic that is solid and fluid at the same time, with a stubborn, insistent beat like a recurring dream; monstrous inventions and unthinkable metamorphoses, sulphurous gleams contrasting with crystalline skies, delicate, rosy nudes face to face with unimaginable freaks of invention intersect or lie in oblique parallels on the vertical plane of pictures in every one of which it seems as though the ritual of the "mating of day and night" were being celebrated, envenomed with the horror of sin and the procreation of monsters.

It is a world that seems far more distant from modern days than the centuries between would warrant; scarcely understandable, even though psychoanalysis can open tiny peep-holes which would certainly not have been necessary to Bosch's contemporaries, for whom these paintings were perfectly decipherable, a mirror and a warning at the same time.

Today, we must look in different ways and from new angles.

The little Brabantine town of 's-Hertogenbosch already reflected all the violent contradictions of that time and those regions. In the vehement struggle between good and evil, between God and the devil, every kind of licence could appear with the fiercest brutality in the most unbridled form.

As Huizinga notes, "even though belief in the devil was directly rooted in a vast deep anguish, yet the imagination of the simple dressed the forms of demons in such gay colours and made them so familiar to all that they ended by losing their terrifying aspect".

As in literature, so in painting: the stink of sulphur and the humours of farce are in the end inextricably confused, and overlaid with sensuality and mysticism.

Ambiguous and distorted, though familiar and accessible to all—this must have been the nature of those popular displays, horrifying scenery and pantomimes, dances with a complicated symbolic meaning, images that were fantastic and intemperate and yet directed towards the edification of the mind through tortuous and unexpected channels, which were performed—some of them with Bosch's co-operation—at 's-Hertogenbosch as they were everywhere. In fact, it was this very Brotherhood of Our Lady, of which the artist was a "notable", which organised them with the same zeal with which it carried out works of charity, and the theme of the temptations of the anchorites must have recurred often in the allegories they showed on their carts.

The Brotherhood of Our Lady was not the only one involved in the restless spiritual, humanistic and visionary humours of 's-Hertogenbosch. The disciples of Gerard Groote, in his turn a follower of Ruysbroeck, united in the community of the Brothers of the Common Life, had opened a school attended for three years by the young Erasmus of Rotterdam. And side by side with societies standing defiantly on the rocky peaks of orthodoxy there were encamped, more or less clandestinely, heretical sects like that of the Free Spirit, the Adamites, some of whom, perhaps, belonged at the same time to the Brotherhood of Our Lady.

And in this connection it is interesting to remember that Fraenger has advanced a strong hypothesis that Bosch was an Adamite, which would clarify and justify the androgyne motifs.

Printing brought a wider distribution of writings on alchemy, and strengthened the fight against sorcery, the fury of which, however, implied a detailed knowledge of these practices; they were finally almost exalted by the Papal Bull of 1484 and by the *Malleus Maleficorum* which condemned them.

In fact, even the strictest Catholic orthodoxy was far from averse to clothing sin in pictures and extremely salacious words, colourfully emphasising its sexual or downright obscene aspects in such a way as to impress the public more vividly and arouse in them a visionary hysteria. As Huizinga also says, even the churches were not free from this licence: displays which might tempt to new and unforeseeable evils were more than tolerated there. Every image, every symbol, every belief was exaggerated and improved upon; they became monstrous, menacing, grotesque.

Dreams, the children of night, took on a prophetic quality; they all meant something. The more freakish the weather, the more possible warnings were read into it. Nature itself was travestied in Bosch's mental vision; the "desert" of the hermits, St Anthony or St Jerome, is not a negation or a cancellation of nature, unthinkable for Nordic man; it is a prison "inside" nature, "within" the evil and menace of nature; thus the forest is deserted by men but populated by terror, because it is a frightening background for mutations and hallucinations. Far away on the horizon there are green plains and blue mountain peaks; side by side with the unending distortion of animals and plants is the precious and corruptible metal of the alchemists.

But among the contradictory components which come from the civilization and culture of Bosch's time to fuse together in his work, and illuminate and colour his paintings in a way entirely peculiar to him, a great part is also played by the moral aspect, the artist's own ethics wrapped up in psychology and symbolism. It is certain that both beyond and within androgyny and hermetic science (which are particularly obvious in *The Hill-man* and *The Alchemical Man*), Bosch reveals himself as an initiate, a man who has tried and "seen many things in order to obtain experience and knowledge of all he wishes to depict".

Under the iron seal of his pictorial language—no less hard to define and clarify than the psychological and cultural elements—his fantastic visions, though always bound up with his symbolic and moral intentions, lead us to postulate exceptional and stimulated dreaming, even the use of drugs—an opinion supported also by certain unaccustomed ways of using colour.

The heightened value given to the senses has almost didactic examples (we need only recall, as far as hearing is concerned, *The Infernal Concert* of the *Triptych of Delights*), the prominence of chalices and cups, the sometimes transparent hints, the food of mysticism, seem to allude to a sort of secular paradise of which the painter knows the ritual: he has been able to "see".

The discovery of natural hallucinogens and the proof that the "witches' ointment" was made and used according to a fifteenth century recipe, lead us to imagine a fantastic world very near to that of Bosch, who must have put his full vitality into a bid for direct knowledge and conscious experience.

Chapter II

THE SECRET WORLD OF BOSCH

The Marriage at Cana (detail)
Boymans van Beuningen Museum, Rotterdam

The first question one might ask when trying to decipher the symbols in Bosch's work is whether he belonged to a sect or secret society.

There is no shortage of elements showing him as an adept; if we examine *The Marriage at Cana* we see at once the signs and symbols of the Lodge. But besides these, we have other reliable references in this very painting. Here we are guided by the research of Fraenger who, after looking into the symbolism of colours and other elements which are, however, open to various interpretations, goes on to analyse the objects appearing in the background on the sideboard, which is the altar of the sorcerer.

According to Castelli, in the two scenes which are going on independently side by side, the two worlds "cannot meet". In the background, by the magic altar, a ceremony is in progress, while servants are bringing in impure foods—the swan and the boar—from which a flame is leaping; a servant, terrified, is about to fall backwards.

But what is happening among those "who are not guests but bondsmen (not free)" goes unnoticed by the guests, while Christ turns the water into wine: a life-giving mystery, while the gesture of the sorcerer, turning the meat into fire, gives nothing.

But in reality, in the foreground of the composition, the "square" arrangement of the table has a clear and primary emphasis which even seems to cancel out the psychological differences of the characters; thus the little red-haired figure standing with its back to us, dressed as a cup-bearer and in the act of offering the cup, seems to suggest a ritual.

Even if the picture is given the significance of a moral lesson and a comment on the passage in St Paul (I Cor. X, 21)—"Ye cannot drink the cup of the Lord, and the cup of devils: ye cannot be partakers of the Lord's table, and of the table of devils"—also expressed through various symbols and by the broad lines of the composition, this, considered one of Bosch's earliest works, already contains elements which betray an acute and perhaps first-hand understanding of esoteric societies and secrets.

If Bosch was an adept, he could still remain faithful to his pledge and to the nature and character of the brotherhood to which he belonged; in fact there is nothing to confirm decisively the suppositions about his belonging to a sect, or the name of it. The Brothers of the Free Spirit? That is Fraenger's supposition. These disciples were, in a way, organised like the members of the Lodges: the gnosis was based on Eros and Agape; they called themselves "brother" and "sister" in the spiritual and the physical sense; sons of Adam, they celebrated the tree and the delights of Paradise. Women had a prominent position, but the cult of the androgyne led to the celebration of Original Man who possessed and united in himself the "masculine solar principle" and the "feminine chthonic (earthy) principle". *The Garden of Delights* appears to reveal the chain of ritual of the sect, even though the meaning of some elements remains obscure: love itself as a rite which presupposes a phase of initiation.

Initiation alters the meanings of the external world and transmutes its appearance, and so finally frees man from the power of suggestion: yet another possibility of "seeing", perhaps also combines with the search for hallucinogenic stimuli.

The Spaniard Father Joseph de Sigüença (1605) provided a very penetrating explanation of Bosch's intent: "As I see it, the difference between the paintings of this man and those of others is this: the others seek to depict men as they appear outwardly; he alone has the audacity to depict them as they are inwardly".

It is, however, obvious that Bosch shows himself to be expert in all fields of esoteric magic, which can help him to break the shell of outward appearance, investing every image with a mysterious wealth of meanings, heightened by a delicate clarity of form.

We may well agree with Combe, according to whom Bosch's basic and dominant themes remain the wiles of the devil and the picture of the human soul exposed to the snares of the Evil One; but all this is flung into the melting-pot with Catholic orthodoxy and heterodox mysticism, occultism and magic, the Cabal and alchemy—knowledge which emanated in all its fervour from the building of cathedrals. And the partly-built cathedral of St John at 's-Hertogenbosch must have been of resounding importance if it was visited later by Dürer. We cannot forget that the "master-builders" of the Cathedral had their headquarters in the House of the Brothood of Our Lady.

Bosch's world appears increasingly bound by links which seem to move in concentric circles; but the ultimate meaning and the distant goal are still out of sight in the loyal secrecy of the adept.

The basic truth about the membership and names of the sects is still uncertain, but it is incontrovertible that Bosch draws from this mysterious source new symbols, new relationships and new laws, in a world which he reshapes through a heightened knowledge of creation which, by descent from heretical theories which see the key to it mainly in sexuality, offers to the mind the bright canvas of the madness of temptation.

The knowledge of creation breathes life into landscapes through two essential components, the alchemical and the mystical, the first of which is predominant.

The key to the universe is the "hermetic mercury" which means possession of nature; it is here that the intimate association of the masculine and feminine elements takes place. Possession is so total and perfect that it can recreate and transmute itself. Consciousness crosses the bounds of outward appearance, and through processes that can be dreamlike and initiatory at the same time, gives shape to a sort of other nature, formed in the reality of the imagination.

In this world the exotic element is also frequent, with a fairy-tale nostalgia for distant unknown lands, and embellished copying of the bestiaries; yet another means of alienation, a suggestion of an unknown paradise.

In *The Garden of Delights* the Fountain of Life exorcises the monsters and promises another kind of existence of which the crystal spheres of alchemical operations are the proof.

The arborescent dreams and the zoomorphic conception of nature have Oriental and Islamic roots; but the illustrated herbaria provided a wonderful store of shapes to elaborate.

Again, we have the glorification of nature and nostalgia for the primal origins. The flower itself offers a quantity of symbols and allusions, such as the cup and the chalice; and fruits are equally full of them, especially when their shape is most perfectly spherical—the cherry, the pumpkin, strawberries and other berries.

The repertory of the bestiary is complex in the same way: the horse, the blackbird, the peacock, the hen, the phoenix, the pelican, the crow. In the alchemist's bestiary the use of colours is very important, and among them black, which indicates the "nigredo", the first stage of the "opus". The search for meanings is infinite, like the wearisome hunt for the philosopher's stone.

An alchemical term brings with it kindred terms and necessitates the accompanying development of meanings. Interpretation is not easy and never definite, but many-sided and

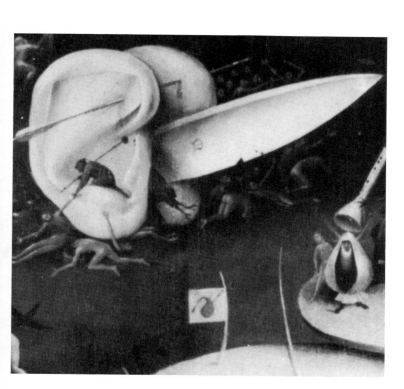

open, and thus ambiguous, following esoteric hermetism and the link with alchemical androgyny, and the double meaning of visions.

The alchemist's bestiary, the occult and magic element, thus become supporting actors in the paintings of temptations and hermits, of St Anthony and St Jerome; the protagonists of the long struggle through the most diverse of sufferings, yet intent, despite everything, on their relationship with God. Their temptations are destined to introduce, by their restlessness and agitation, compositional and narrative elements which exclude any traditional imagery.

The saint does not contemplate with a sort of detachment the origin and manner of his torments; he participates, suffers, accepts every moment of this demoniacal ritual; in it he has lost—or it appears secondary or swallowed up in the whole—even the animal which accompanies and characterises him (the lamb for John the Baptist, the lion for Jerome); but all beasts, plants and flowers, the hybrids and minerals, recreate for him a menacing land of prophecy, the torture of an unknown or forgotten world which he has to accept as the "other" realm of nature.

In this world the human figure and its individual parts and gestures demand particular attention, like the ear (see, for example, *The Garden of Delights*) which not only confirms an obsession with the erotic, but supplements the eye and such alchemical signs as the closed mouth in ensuring that no transgression will be committed. It is another proof of esoteric secrecy, like the powers of irradiation and reception given by the Magi to the body's extremities: the top of the head, the feet and hands. From this it is but a step to the possibility of communication and transference of magic in a series of gestures that accentuate the esoterism.

It is probable that the gesture is a beckoning one: "an invitation to nothing" (Castelli) although everything seems to point to the belief that there is a hidden world which merits discovery. *Ignoti nulla cupido:* the unknown is not desirable just because it is unknown. But in the gesture of a tempting demon is the promise of desire for the unknown, and the interlinked and unsatisfied questions that it brings with it. That is why the Ghent St Jerome, having taken off his cardinal's robes, prostrate on the rock and clutching the crucifix, prays with closed eyes to avoid being attracted by the gesture of temptation.

But pagan mythology cannot be discounted either in Bosch's fantastic world; light is the attribute of Apollo, god of the arts and also of divination. An appeal to pagan images is seen in the symbols of the lyre and the dolphin, the lizard and the griffon.

This incessant ebb and flow of symbols is present in Bosch's paintings as in every sectarian rite: every current and every vector finds its place there until it is firmly entrenched and generates hybrids whose meaning is debatable.

All sources before Christianity and before the affirmation of dogma introduce elements of contrast and even of contest; the owl is a symbol of a particular wisdom, the science which penetrates the invisible.

Thus heterodoxy, fed by esoterism, can give the symbols their meaning, and the initiate is of necessity a visionary.

We can also understand, in this context, the spatial construction of many of Bosch's paintings, which have a disconcerting mobility which never pauses from its symbols and meanings, but looks for its own self-formed and self-justificatory nucleus in the central theme, generally to do with the lives of the saints or other such subjects so that any objections to other elements

in the pictures will be overshadowed by the moral theme. But from there, themes radiate in apparent visual disorder, but in reality according to a sustained allusive logic; they are refracted and seem to stand out with a metallic sharpness, finding in their meetings and interweavings the most plausible significance.

This space, at first probed as one might look for edification into a mirror, becomes the scene of vital events the possible extensions of which it multiples and dilates almost magically by the insidious introduction of sub-themes.

In these spaces, in backgrounds and landscapes, Bosch restates over and over again his passion for architecture. In Bosch, a whole city can be understood through its architecture. In opposition to elements which take on a symbolic meaning—like the unfinished house or the tumbledown hovel, which may be allusions to the Old Testament—the painter gives obvious importance to the profiles of cities; not only when, detached against the blaze of the fire, the buildings make a last stand against the final punishment (a reference to Sodom and Gomorrah?) but even more when the cities spread out their towers against the clear skies of Brabant according to a design which seems even to bear some relation to town-planning—or at least to an ideal town-planning—in the sense that the city is seen as essentially fitting into man's existence: a focal point of primary interest.

If certain towns appearing in the background represent 's-Hertogenbosch, that town is, for Bosch, a New Jerusalem, penetrated by the theosophical science of the Chaldean Magi. The Orient, first Jewish and then Islamised, had a strong attraction for Bosch; Jewish thought, together with contemporary and earlier currents of mysticism and esoterism, form an apparently contradictory triad which is resolved in the fabric of images and symbols.

In the pre-Reformation environment in which the Renaissance began to take shape in the Netherlands, every interpolation and every reference gave life to the many figurative and divinatory humours, while the rebirth of Judaism also renewed interest in numbers, because Rabbinical interpretation of the Scriptures used methods in which letters had a mathematical function.

But if architecture re-enters the science of numbers, so, no less, does the art of music. Every one of Bosch's paintings has its own mysterious and paradoxical orchestration. In *The Garden of Delights* the *Infernal Concert* shows an enormous quantity and variety of instruments, some of which seem to be related to instruments of torture.

But though music may generate harmony and have cathartic powers, in the same way the monotonous repetition of one rhythm may lead to a hallucinatory state of psychic suspension, just as an excess of sound, where all the instruments are used at maximum power and intensity, may overtake and wipe out the purifying effect of music. And here again interpretation loses itself in a complexity that is perhaps insoluble.

At other times the magic meanings that Bosch gives to signs and images are more transparent, especially when some elements show recurring references to initiation, for example the two women in *The Garden of Delights* who have shaven heads and who, according to Fraenger, are "initiates, as the leaves adorning their heads indicate". Often nakedness has a magic significance, like the ritual nakedness of Adam or the partial nudity which indicates precisely the quality of initiate: the shoulders of the Judaic Messiah, the knee of the Prodigal Son or of the Wandering Fool.

Other symbols of the hermetic tradition—

Triptych of the Garden of Delights
The Garden of Delights (detail)
Prado, Madrid

besides various signs of initiation most evident, for example, in *The Marriage at Cana* and less apparent in the details of the Venice *Triptych of the Hermits*—are hidden in Bosch's works: the tree and the serpent refer to woman, to Eve; the windmill and the weathervane indicate the element of air, and are alchemical signs; and then the planets, the staircase, the mirror, and the fools who are certainly not there to increase the number in the crowd scenes, but must have a particular justification for appearing.

On the other hand, the dense human population which appears side by side with the animals and the hybrids in Bosch's paintings seems to reflect an intelligent and real participation in this "underground learning" which the painter could depict and glorify, sure of being understood.

If he always worked in 's-Hertogenbosch, this spiritual centre must of necessity have been inhabited by people who were far from ignorant of this learning, to whose demands the figurative and symbolic designs responded, and were thus completely legible.

All the culture of the period filters into this pictorial work: not only that which comes from arcane sciences, but also that which is spread by public ceremonies and popular festivals. As we also find in Huizinga's studies, in that "Autumn of the Middle Ages", in the conflict between spiritual and temporal power, festivals were encouraged and even promoted by the authorities, who saw in recreational pursuits a means of making the people more docile and malleable. Even festivals could be a means of popularisation. In a spiritual centre like 's-Hertogenbosch, the people would have known about initiation, and would have been ready to pass on this knowledge and so the function of Bosch's art was to remind or to open the way to the initiate's ability to "see".

Once again, at the dawn of this new era immediately preceding the Reformation, the return to Jewish studies and to all pre-Christian culture led to the visionary exaltation of a sort of "topsy-turvy" world of which we have only a few key elements, but which asserts itself above all in its overwhelming fantastic reality; a world which has a certain satirical vein belonging naturally to pre-Reformation trends, but which Tolnay supposes to be described by Bosch *con amore*; a world in which, however, the clash can be felt between history which is consecrated and recognised, and thus considered objective, and the history of oral tradition. The source of knowledge becomes increasingly contradictory; the authenticity of an event or an action may be difficult to establish.

The relationships of men with God is illustrated by the terrible experiences of the hermits (St Anthony, St Jerome, John the Baptist); their struggles and victories are set against the agitation and turmoil of unbelief shown by the array of magic signs and alchemical symbols. Many paintings, with their interweaving of Judaic, mystic and pagan themes, seem intened to stimulate the intellect.

A mental geography that is fabulous, yet true on the initiate's plane, comes from the Eastern lands, first Jewish, then converted to Islam. Contradictory exotic elements invade the field, together with mysterious elements and symbols with which Bosch always reveals a subtle familiarity. But his knowledge of the contemporary stage and of masques gave rise to his contorted images and monsters.

In the Prado *Triptych of the Epiphany* the problems of interpretation cannot have one single solution; is it an image of the struggle between Christ and Antichrist, or an ambiguous quarrel between the new law and the old, or a reflection of the service offered to the Virgin by the Brotherhood of Our Lady? Even in one of Bosch's clearest paintings the interpretation seems to be a matter for controversy.

Chapter III

TRADITION AND SYMBOLISM

Triptych of the Garden of Delights
The Garden of Delights (detail)
Prado, Madrid

In Bosch's visionary universe the chief feature is the symbol; whether traditional and associated with the lives of the saints or drawn from the occult sciences.

Oral tradition meets, and is finally absorbed by, spiritual thought and mystical practices, all alive and fermenting in a town like 's-Hertogenbosch "impregnated with the manners and customs, the ways of thought and action, that belonged to the mediaeval world"; a centre, then, which gave a spiritual explorer like Bosch the chance to have his own extraordinary experiences.

All this has its meeting point in the work of art. If, as Castelli asserts, Bosch's paintings denounce magic and the wiles of the Evil One, it is also true that the painter shows himself to be steeped in arcane knowledge which he transmits through symbolic images to the initiates and also to those who are striving towards that knowledge.

Nothing appears without meaning or in a purely anecdotal vein; every element is part of the grammar of a mysterious language, comprehensible to those who know. These people were also familiar with already known sources of images which were partly used by Bosch: the *Visio Tundali*, the *Ars Moriendi*, the *Grand Calendrier des Bergers*, the *Biblia Pauperum*; sources which, together with those of the initiates, were an essential contribution to the literature on this subject.

Every image had thus its own meaning, either primary and open, or more secret, or even actually occult. For example, the display of birds in *The Garden of Delights* may be connected with the symbol of a bird perched on Adam's arm in *The Vision of Beyond*, which seems to be delivering a message, since birds symbolise angels. Thus imagination alone does not give enough help to the observer, nor does hagiography, because images can be derived from several different sources.

And since in every Bosch painting, even in those easiest to decipher, the visionary element is a basic component, the type and origin of such "visions" have been precisely investigated.

It is true that Tolnay had already hinted at dream phenomena and psychoanalytical processes, but suppositions have invaded even more mysterious fields, such as the taking of substances like fungi or fresh herbs, not to mention the more or less legendary "witches' ointment", made of vegetable ingredients. The hallucinatory effects produced by substances unknown today, which may perhaps have come to the northern ports from distant countries, must have caused terrible dreams, similar to those which began the initiate's ordeals. But in the vision, the space given to experience, visual and otherwise, expands until it leads to a view of the cosmos which is not dogmatic.

In this context the relationship between temptation and vision also plays a prominent part. In fact the hermit, having retreated from the world and living alone in his holy place, mortified by privations and lack of sleep and by the food he eats (for example, water and bread made of spurred rye, the hallucinatory effect of which has been proved) is fertile ground for ecstasy and visions; hence the extraordinary, overwhelming variety of images which he sees, and of which Bosch's work shows an astonishing selection, in which the analogical references appear more and more rich and various. By identifying a few dominant themes it is possible to verify the symbolic links and thus find a guide to comprehension.

The problem at this point is to decide how much of the mystical vision is comprised in Bosch's imaginary world; or whether, in denouncing magic and trickery, the profound knowledge of the very arguments denounced is not imposing itself irresistibly on the other aspects of the painter's art. It is certain, however, that conscious fidelity to the *Corpus Hermeticum* governs in the artist the obvious choice of signs and symbols and alchemical images. There is an infinite number of indications of this, and it is sufficient to consult the basic evidence found in *The Garden of Delights*.

The scenes showing temptations and visions are also full of magic and caballistic ciphers which create a pervasive sense of antithesis and imbalance with regard to the hagiographic aspect of the ascetic life. Orthodoxy thus appears threatened from within by the assaults of unbelief and heterodoxy.

On the other hand, every vein of unbelief is fed by the fascinating influx of pagan antiquity which at the transition between the Middle Ages and the Renaissance, was well able to take root between the intellectual attractions of theology on one side and hermetism on the other. The close ties between these different components have been especially brought to light in the last few years by studies on *The Alchemical Man* and on the *Melancholy* of Dürer. Bosch's cryptography is not smugly closed in on itself; it is an invitation to enquiry, to meditation on the allusive logic of its analogies until we can see far beyond appearances, to the very limits of meaning; and the secular part of Bosch's altarpieces, even if their point is hagiographic or moral, actually consists of a didactic statement.

But in the fabric of temptation and vision the basic element is the apparent negation of logical order; the rule of chaos. In the images and in the development of symbols everything is topsy-turvy; the irrational is a snare and a negation; and even the temptations and punishments seem to imply a sort of complaisant masochism rather than spiritual redemption.

Temptations or diabolical tortures, the demonstrations of the orgiastic host override the narrative motifs taken for edification from the *Legenda Aurea* or the *Vitae Patrum*: in those desert wastes every aspect of paganism can invade and prevail.

Even one of the most fascinating and pictorially perfect images, such as the female nude, has its roots in pagan antiquity, just as, in part anyway, it has its justification for the initiate.

The female nude, taut, agile and firm, delicate in colour almost to transparency, is artistically one of the most perfect features of Bosch's work, while from the symbolic point of view it contains one of the fundamental demoniacal elements.

The nude and the tree lead us to the idea of Eve, but at the same time the tree symbolises female fertility, and the nude emerging from the hollow tree recalls the mythological image of the Dryads, the nymphs who lived in hollow trees, or perhaps even a primitive cult connected with Artemis, who is shown on a coin from Myra with Aphrodite inside a hollow trunk.

However, the nude emerging from a tree is also an alchemical image, and this appeal to symbolism, made more complex by the presence of a male so as to represent a coupling of the alchemical type, fire and water, appears in the figure of a woman coming into view in the left-hand panel of the *Altar piece of the Hermits*, standing, moreover, with her legs in water up to the knees—a part of the body important in initiation rites.

If Bosch gives so much artistic and symbolic importance to the female nude, it is also obvious that as a physical type it is elongated in the Gothic style, according to the canons of feminine beauty which must have predominated at 's-Hertogenbosch. But the painter always gives this type of woman the diabolical role of temptress, like the Greek Aphrodite or the Roman Venus. And at the same time, her power is fertilising and regenerative so that in the midst of a Sabbat of monsters and oddities, visionary anguish and incredible happenings, there are unexpected patches of the tender green of a Spring landscape; perhaps no less menacing, if they are cunning alternatives to the temptations of man —if in this cosmogony outside dogma, pagan tradition is stating the powers of Venus in the fruitful union of heaven and earth.

Chapter IV

REALITY AND IMAGINATION

Up to now it has perhaps been possible to bring out something which will be more fully confirmed while examining Bosch's principal paintings: that is, that the variety of images, their immense scope for analogy and their symbolic references are arranged in every picture in accordance with a complex thematic pattern. The identification of these themes can therefore be one of the most enlightening guides to Bosch's meaning.

According to various critical and explanatory trends, Bosch's work can appear to be solely the reflection of an "underground learning" solidly in the possession of the artist and comprehensible to a large number of his fellow-citizens. Yet he may have wanted to show the diabolical desolation of a world outside the sphere of Grace, using his mysterious crytography to serve in the struggle against every form of evil. At any rate, he reveals a direct knowledge of all the possibilities of deception and through it expresses his world which could even be that of a moralist. It is almost like the imaginative and allusive words of St Mechthild: "There is a heaven which the devil builds with his alluring arts. There, thoughts are errant, and the senses sad, and the soul is silent because it cannot find that to which its nature aspires".

The complex fabric of Bosch's symbolic allusions thus needs various methods of interpretation, necessary every time there is any other example of "fantastic art" to be deciphered. And it is certain that for a more reliable interpretation we would need the sum total of all the arcane knowledge on which Bosch's universe is fed, in order to find instruments sharp enough to penetrate the aims and reasons of this crytography.

The same mass of knowledge is equally necessary for understanding many paintings by

Leonardo, Giorgione and Bruegel, Holbein and Cranach, and, obviously, Dürer; the recent essay by Calvesi on the *Melancholia* is a fundamental example of this; it opens new perspectives for the study of analogous problems.

Bosch's cultural, intellectual and spiritual constituents are extremely complex, and his self-expression can be read on different occasions as that of a heresiarch or a moralist; but the origin and elaboration of his dominant themes is more complex still. For the very reason that everything appears to converge on one particular vision of the world, the reasons for this vision remain obscure.

Attempts have been made to list Bosch's themes and the chapter on signs and symbols at the end of this book gives a brief guide to these themes.

Every piece of research done on this appears limited once it is put into close contact with the interpretation of the paintings. For example, even the recent work of Tolnay on the dream-symbols according to Freud appears incomplete, while that made by Fraenger for *The Marriage at Cana* is limited to one small sector; this painting is enclosed in a difficult hermetism, an essential foundation not only for the specific understanding of the work itself but for the interpretation of many of Bosch's paintings.

The meanings of many symbols are still obscure and thus an exhaustive catalogue of their meanings cannot be provided; examination of the principal works which are unmistakably marked with the painter's own style, may help with the comparison between opposing inter-pretations. However, we today are hampered because we do not possess that learning through which Bosch was able to communicate with his contemporaries.

Chapter V

THE ART OF BOSCH

If we think of an artist who has always lived in a little place like 's-Hertogenbosch, we might expect his provincial origins to come out in his art. However, although deeply rooted in a civilization of late mediaeval stamp, 's-Hertogenbosch was a progressive cultural centre and Bosch had certainly no lack of poetical, philosophical and visual inspiration. It was in this humus that his painting fermented—a language woven of particular experiences, avoiding all conventional patterns and making of him, as Tolnay says, a "universal artist". We cannot underestimate, in that area of Europe, the cultural supremacy maintained by the northern regions against the southern ones, or, in that pre-Reformation climate, Bosch's constant effort to evade the dogmatic rigidity of the religious authorities and to uphold intellectual freedom.

In this attempt at individual redemption lies the friction caused by all the contradictions of his time, all the more evident by the fact that every one of Bosch's subjects—even those apparently profane—is an enquiry into a religious theme, dramatic in all its paradoxes and yet religious in its wealth of meanings and variations. And however personal the problems faced in every painting may at first appear, it is —as can be seen in individual cases—the very complexity of actions and reactions called forth in every picture which brings out the most various and profoundly true aspects of humanity. This humanity Bosch explores and considers in all the dynamism of impulse and the logic of behaviour.

The soul of the picture is in its colour; and the greatest possible care goes into the choice of the tone-register, since the value of the symbol lies in the dominant colours and their relationships, in contrasts and monochromes.

Colour does not only translate and heighten meanings by strengthening their analogies—it is sufficient to think of the tender subtle shades of *The Garden of Delights* and the moist landscapes of the background; the intense, concentrated colours of *The Cure for Madness*, contrasted with white and grey; the red of *The Conjuror* and the sulphurous mist of *Ecce Homo*; the green of the impossible landing-place of *The Ship of Fools*; the delicately shaded garments of *St John on Patmos*, and the metallic transparency of the rocks; the pointed symbolism of the colours in *The Marriage at Cana*—but the colour itself accentuates the dynamism of the conflicts, lights up the swirling motion of the figures, and expands or contracts space itself.

When colour is thus used to obtain a precise effect, design comes first. Bosch left sketches and studies for paintings, and sketchbook pages thickly covered with the "monsters" of his imagination, and in the paintings themselves the design analyses the image, faithfully transcribing his extraordinary imaginative visions, the distortions, the strange shapes and unexpected combinations, with clear and accurate strokes, within which the colour seems to take its place as though it were part of an alchemical process.

Bosch's graphic exploration into his universe thus becomes the faithful transcription of the probings of his intellect, the first statement of an operation which is carried on in a constant state of inventive tension.

But these are not the only diversive elements which intensify and multiply the focal points of interpretation; these also arise from places, landscapes or buildings, either real or imaginary, but which lead to direct intuitions of psychological value; or they are even warnings, as in the case of sexual actions, tortures or monstrosities which on the one hand accentuate the sense of alienation and, on the other, give the observer an insight into Bosch's moral attitude. Bosch also gives great importance to glances between people, to the way they cross, evade each other and are lost, and this stimulates the observer to unravel the complex messages in his work. As Sedlmayr remarked, neither space nor time remain constant in Bosch; their convulsive disintegration and dispersion takes place in a dimension which is "infra-naturalistic". Here even places and distances appear in extraordinary relief, mainly because they are governed by the laws of the absurd and are fixed according to another opposing order which can best be described as anti-nature.

The personal psychological element in Bosch's work should not be underestimated. His paintings of the spiritual ordeals of the hermits and the temptations of the flesh have an emotional impact which can only come from his own personal experience. As Fraenger remarks, only a man who has been strongly tempted can plunge himself utterly into the depths of emotion and communicate the experience of that temptation.

Chapter VI

A SELF-PORTRAIT OF BOSCH AND CHRONOLOGY OF HIS WORKS

We have little documentary evidence to help us unravel the secret of Bosch's life, which can be only partly reconstructed through research into the culture and customs of the time and place in which he lived. His work, moreover, allows of surprising interpretations and provides biographical information which enables us to build up the image of a unique personality. It is possible to gain some idea of the artist through the self-portrait in the Bibliothèque de la Ville d'Arras, a rough sketch as far as the clothes are concerned, but sharp and penetrating in the drawing of the face, that of a shrewd, mature man, with wide-set eyes and an asymmetrical, disconcerting look, the nose long and fleshy, the thin lips giving firmness to the mouth. Some say the drawing is a later copy, "but of good quality".

Other scholars have tried to identify the artist's own portrait in his paintings; for example Baldass thinks that the figure at the bottom left of the *Christ Carrying the Cross* in Vienna, behind the soldier in armour, is a self-portrait; Baldass and Tolnay think the same of the layman helping to lead the exhausted hermit in the left-hand panel of the Lisbon *Temptations of St Anthony*, with his knee uncovered in the partial nudity of the initiate. The head of *The Alchemical Man* in *The Infernal Concert* of *The Garden of Delights* is generally considered to be a self-portrait, and the drawing of the *Tree-man* in the Albertine Gallery, Vienna, is considered by Tolnay, Baldass and Combe to be an authentic preliminary sketch.

But the hallucinated reality of Bosch's world is not so easily traceable in this portrait sketch as in his works; though even with regard to them and their chronology there is no lack of problems and mysteries.

It is therefore necessary to reconstruct the sequence of these paintings not so much by

themes, but as far as possible in the context of a development in time, in which the dominant images and symbols can take their place in the complete fabric which we need in order to know Bosch's intentions.

In spite of the fact that there are neither dates nor documentary references, Bosch scholars have tried to fix the sequence of the works according to a logical scheme of development based on observation and analysis of pictorial elements and intentions, subdividing the paintings approximately into the three main periods of youth, maturity and old age.

There is no doubt that in the first period the composition is still rather awkwardly planned. The motifs which were to dominate in the middle period appear in embryo, although the painter is already receptive to all those sources which he will later investigate and elaborate thoroughly.

The second period is that of the great compositions and most famous triptychs. The technique is more polished and more suitable to the subject; everything is concentrated on throwing into relief the complex meanings. Space shows depths which are not entirely plumbed, because he uses bands of images arranged freely but carefully, with a slightly oblique movement to give the effect of a dream sequence.

As we have said about the design, all the work of Bosch's final period is marked by a more conscious simplification which tends to arrange the images in sober but very effective frames.

In trying to date the three periods of work, we may rely mainly on Tolnay: 1475–80; 1480–1510; 1510–16; while Combe suggests some modifications to this plan, placing his youthful works between 1475 and 1485; those of his maturity between 1485 and 1505, and the late works between 1505 and 1516.

Recently Cinotti has attempted to pinpoint his periods of work still more accurately: the

Triptych of the Garden of Delights
The Garden of Delights (detail)
Prado, Madrid

Christ Carrying the Cross (detail)
Kunsthistorisches Museum, Vienna

Christ Carrying the Cross (detail)
Kunsthistorisches Museum, Vienna

first youthful period (see for example *The Cure
for Folly, The Marriage at Cana, The Conjuror*)
between 1475 and 1480, linking it with international Gothic and a form that is "plain, static,
but already full of inner strength"; the second
youthful period 1480–85 (see the Brussels *Crucifixion*, the Philadelphia *Epiphany*, the Frankfurt
Ecce Homo) which seeks in various directions
for "the possibility of an angular movement";
the first mature period, 1485–1500 (see *The Ship
of Fools* or the Vienna *Christ Carrying the Cross*)
during which the figures appear small and
crowded, arranged from bottom to top, culminating in *The Haywain*; the second mature
period, 1500–1510, is richer in colour and more
complex, the period of the great triptychs like
that of the *Delights* or the Lisbon *Temptations*
in which intense spatial, pictorial and formal
problems appear, tending finally to subside, or
at least to seek a solution to the most crucial
contradictions, in the late period, from 1508–10
until his death; a period from which the most
enigmatic example is the Prado *Epiphany*.

Cinotti confirms her research mainly through
historical records and critical analysis, but
Tolnay has tried to make a thematic sequence,
psychological and poetic at the same time,
coincide with the chronological one: the paintings which are a "mirror of the world" between
1475 and 1480; those of the "sufferings of the
Saviour", the "detachment from the world" and
the "ascetic life" between 1480 and 1510; and
finally the "ultimate synthesis" between 1510
and 1516.

But apart from these various details and a
few observations which will be necessary when
we examine the works, the chronological
sequence as a whole is generally accepted by all
scholars; and it is in this sequence that we shall
choose the paintings which we consider fundamental for the understanding of the painter of
's-Hertogenbosch.

Chapter VII

THE MAJOR WORKS OF ART

Pictorial, symbolic and moral values are so subtly interwoven in Bosch's work that it is difficult to show how these elements all meet together in the unity of his painting; and yet it is dangerous to attempt to isolate them, allotting a sort of hierarchical importance to one aspect or another. His language develops and matures and his means of expression increase and become more polished, not by means of a movement from simplicity to complexity or vice versa, but according to an inner logic replying to the painter's moral and spiritual demands.

Thus all the meeting points come together in a dense fabric in which Bosch's stylistic independence comes close to the Dutch style, as in the paintings of Dirk Bouts and Geertgen, members of the Haarlem circle, from which he could derive a vein of solemn lyricism, or the realism displayed in the lightness of the images. Perhaps he was interested too in the sort of expressionism used by a prolific painter of Delft, called the Master of the Virgo inter Virgines, while as far as Flemish painting is concerned, Bosch's stylistic independence sometimes shows evidence of contact with the Master of Flémalle, or the vastness of van Eyck's natural landscapes.

His first works were certainly helped by reference to great contemporary or slightly earlier painting, like a rich colouring of 'international" origins: but Bosch was already trying to modify these borrowings with a more direct and popular view of reality.

All this is already evident in a work almost unanimously considered as among the first: *The Cure for Folly* (Prado, Madrid; there are four copies, of which the best is at the Rijksmuseum, Amsterdam). This little picture, which can be dated 1475–80, has at the top and bottom an inscription in Gothic characters: "*Meester snyt die keye ras / Myne name is Lubbert Das*", which means: "Master, cut out the stone quickly

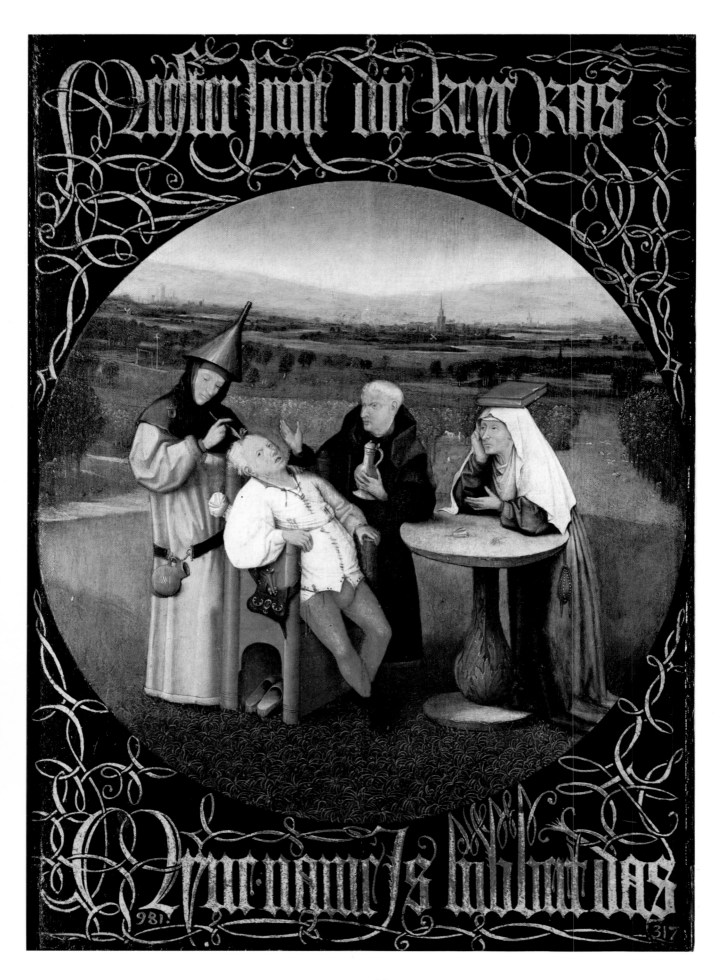

The Cure for Folly p. 44
Prado, Madrid

The Cure for Folly (detail)
Prado, Madrid

The Cure for Folly (detail)
Prado, Madrid

/ My name is Lubbert Das". The last words can be translated something like "simple", "fool", "ignorant." The caption clearly refers to the composition: the character awkwardly seated is submitting to the strange operation with servile credulity, while the monk seems to be encouraging him and the nun gazes into the distance, her elbows on the table, a closed book on her head: science is useless for this disease, and so the volume is balanced precariously, and the woman is present at the action but takes no part in it. That the man tricking "Lubbert Das" is a quack doctor is shown by the funnel on his head, symbol of deceit, while the patient's purse is transfixed by a dagger, indicating that the only one who benefits from the operation is the quack surgeon, who is doing it for money. From the wound emerges a flower, and another flower, a tulip, symbol of madness, is on the table-top. According to Erasmus, medicine is "the art which is closest to madness" and the bitter joke played on a credulous fool shows the vanity of that art; Bosch must have been echoing popular beliefs and the substance of certain sermons. Here the allusions are simple and comprehensible, or lost in the vastness of the background, like the wheel of torture or the gallows, in a landscape placed in a circle, almost in a receding hollow.

This quest for an optical arrangement which can be identified with a sort of eye, the mirror of the world, the "mandala" of meditation, is obvious in *The Seven Deadly Sins* (1475–80, Prado, Madrid). In the iris is the image of Christ, from which shine an infinite number of rays, and which is thus identified with the sun; in the "cornea" (which for Tolnay and Combe represents the globe), in trapezoidal sections, are shown examples of the seven deadly sins. At the corners of the "eye" four discs show the Last Judgment: Death and Judgment, Hell and

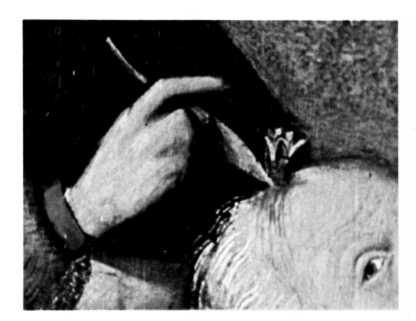

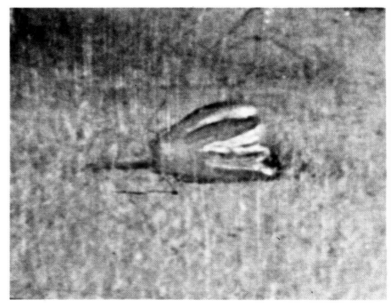

Heaven. These circles re-echo mediaeval images familiar to Bosch's public, and the furious physical retribution of Hell or the edifying hierarchy of the Elect would be enough for them. But the lesson becomes still more intense and directly understood through the example of the sins: brilliantly effective scenes interpreted by figures dressed in the costume of the time, engaged in every excess, in the streets of their city or inside their houses, faithfully reconstructed and shown with domestic familiarity, with clear-cut outlines and a softness of colour recalling examples of the Haarlem school, or, in the Pride section, seeming even to allude to van Eyck's portrait of the *Arnolfini*, by the use of perspective and the functon of the mirror, here held by a devil. But even the allusions are recurrent; the reflection of the world is cruel and baleful, despite the sun-like iris, the clear sky, the moist and tender colours, the narrative quality of the scenes. A similar picture is *The Conjuror* (1475–

80, Saint-Germain-en-Laye, Municipal Museum), a recurring episode in provincial life, but at the same time a moralistic and admonitory theme: the charlatan is playing on the credulity of fools. Here the horizon is restricted, closed by a high wall; in this narrow sphere the charlatan's robe blazes with colour; he is diabolically isolated, directing at his pleasure human stupidity characterised by the types in his audience, but especially typified in the man who is "spitting toads" on the table, while a neighbour is stealing his purse and a boy is mocking him. There are plenty of more subtle interpretations giving a foretaste of symbols to be found later in Bosch's more mature images; thus for Combe, the owl in the conjuror's basket is a symbol of the heresy which attracts minds not supported by the Christian faith, while he identifies the conjuror himself with the First Major Arcana of the Tarot, that is to say, with the one who, in hermetic language, aspires to create on a level with God, as shown

by the magic wand he holds in his hand.

At any rate, whatever the most apt interpretations may be, before reaching the complexity of the heretical ritual suggested by Fraenger, Bosch shows a firmer, more definite type of composition. The bystanders' positions are static, but there is movement in the expressive tension of the faces, in the curve described by the credulous demonstrator, in the arrangement of the figures, which seems to press at the barrier of the wall, in the use of colours against black; finally everything is resolved in the magical suggestion of the table-top, large in comparison with the wretched instruments on it, and the isolation of the charlatan: an already clever example of the controlling use of allusion.

But the best example of a painting with many interpretations, which at first glance may seem easily decipherable, but which becomes complicated and even manic on closer investigation, is *The Marriage at Cana* (1475–80, Rotterdam, Boymans—van Beuningen Museum).

We must say at once that the picture has suffered two cuts at the top corners, and has been much restored, especially the heads which have almost all been repainted; the two dogs were added in the eighteenth century. It may be true, as Tolnay says, that the L-shaped table recalls the Giottoesque design of the *Scrovegni*, but a certain resemblance, in the solemn rigidity of the figures, to the *Last Supper* of Dirk Bouts (Louvain, St Peter's) is more evident still. However, apart from these resemblances, Bosch introduces into his composition, inspired by the well-known passage from the Gospels, an atmosphere of unease which does not come so much from the slanting perspective—it is actually mitigated by the suffusion of colour which binds the images one to another much more than narrative or episodic links—but is pointed by every significant detail; a hard test for scholars'

interpretative abilities. It results "from the double meaning attached to the basic theme, already complex, and the symbolic value which is consequently attributed to the scene". The careful observer cannot but see that, as in other works of Bosch, the composition offers various keys to the code, disturbingly full as it is of symbolic and esoteric details and demoniacal and magical allusions.

Under the canopy, against a gilded wall in the Islamic style, are Christ and the donor, a little separate from the rest of the guests, including the Madonna and the bride, who sit motionless and abstracted along the sides of the table, while at the ends couples are talking together, almost indifferent to Christ's gesture. He is making the sign of benediction—of what? The turning of water into wine? or perhaps rather the cup held by the strange red-haired figure seen from behind, small but authoritative (the chair destined for him is the one richly inlaid with gold) who is very clearly wearing the distinctive sign of the knotted sash? The boy may be one of the main threads of Bosch's cryptogram.

Let us once more attempt to interpret this picture, rich in magic.

The table is L-shaped, perhaps alluding to the symbols of the Lodges, and the little red-haired character has the sign of his authority in the sash; the cup, at the intersection point of the diagonals, may indicate the preparation of a drink connected with the celebration of mysteries. His face is not turned to Christ, nor to either of the principal women guests, the Madonna and the bride; his gaze is fixed directly on the sideboard.

In reality the miracle appears to be taking place in a general atmosphere of inattention, since besides the distraction of the animated couples, there is interest attached to other actions taking place behind the backs of the

The Marriage at Cana (detail)
Musée Boymans van Beuningen, Rotterdam

The Marriage at Cana (detail)
Musée Boymans van Beuningen, Rotterdam

The Marriage at Cana (detail)
Musee Boymans van Beuningen, Rotterdam

guests, the probable significance of which seems to be connected with the presence of the mysterious boy.

On a high platform a musician is entertaining the guests with a tune on the bagpipes, an impious instrument with sexual connotations, while on top of a column a strange little moon-devil is shooting an arrow at his companion who is escaping through a hole in the wall above the side column. The servants are bringing in the food, a wild boar and a swan; these too are impure, even the swan, regarding which Combe mentions the interpretation of the fourteenth century mystics, according to whom it was a symbol of dissipation and hypocrisy ("white without, black within") all the more because it wears on its breast the half-moon of heresy. On the other hand, the swan was a choice dish at the banquets of the Brotherhoods; it is known to have been eaten at the one in which Bosch took part (1488) to celebrate his admission to the Brotherhood of Our Lady.

However, the effects of these dishes are evil; from them springs the fire which is terrifying the servant who has come to carry the trays, and perhaps striking him to the ground. But all this is going on behind the guests' backs and almost without their knowledge, as though opposing the world of truth to the world of heresy, grace to the work of the devil. In fact, as we have said, the boy in ritual dress is looking at the sideboard in the background, beside which stands the Master of Ceremonies. Or a magus? Not only does the wand he is holding appear to support this hypothesis, but also the meaning of the objects on the shelf of the sideboard, which is thus transformed into an altar of magic. One explanation might identify objects relative to Christian liturgy like the bread, the jugs, the statuette of St Christopher with the weight of the globe on his bent shoulders, the pelican,

symbol of Christ, as opposed to lust, identifiable in the dancing nudes, and heresy, symbolised, according to Combe, by the sea urchin at the summit of this sort of "ziggurat".

But with regard to these objects and the meanings they can assume, Fraenger—who suggests an interpretation of the entire painting based on astrological and heretical symbols, and believes that the marriage refers to that of the Jew Jacob de Almaengien, Master of the Brotherhood of the Free Spirit, who, according to Fraenger, commissioned Bosch's strangest and most hermetic paintings (it is certainly known that he belonged to the Brotherhood of Our Lady, but later returned to his original religion) —makes a very detailed analysis: the ochre colour of the altar of the magus is considered symbolic of mother earth; inside the space enclosed by four columns representing the cardinal points and the elements, the three altar-steps represent the zones of the body, the mind and the spirit, over which the canopy is the emblem of the ultra-lunar world. Fraenger's analysis is certainly not as brief as that; it takes into account every tiny detail and finds a general idea reflected in each of them

For Fraenger, the object at which the magus's wand is pointing is not bread, but a breast, the symbol of female fertility, and the little bronze pot on the left refers to the alchemist's crucible, while the ibis, beating its wings, indicates death untamed by the redemption of the created world; the black jugs on the right signify matter formed into the shape of man. The analysis continues—not entirely improbable, especially for some of the meanings given—until the fine veil falling from above on to the altar is interpreted as the fluid which "on one hand guides the spirit to become one with the earth, and on the other raises it up to blend with the heavens".

Christt and the Woman taken in Adultery
Museum of Art, Philadelphia

Heads of Priests
Musée Boymans van Beuningen, Rotterdam

The hypothesis has also been advanced (Se Solier) that the whole scene alludes to a foundation banquet, an esoteric rite in which the sideboard in the background is a Gnostic altar, over which the ribbed vault, suggesting a church, might explain the origin and existence of certain forms of faith: in that case, could this be a Manichaen initiation?

But whatever may be the particular and subtle meanings attributed to this work—an example that goes to show that an interpretation based on brief references or iconographical schemes is not enough to explain the emblematic world of Bosch—it is certain that the problem of symbols involves the entire composition and throws a new, arcane light on all the guests, their gestures and their dress, so that the artist's language affirms a complex unity of its own, "sweeping into an enigmatic diapason even the apparently logical elements of the story" (Cinotti).

From the point of view most closely related to the pictorial language, this work can be connected with the *Two Heads of Priests* (Rotterdam, Boymans—van Beuningen Museum) especially by the facial characterisation accentuated by the wicked features, and another composition inspired by a passage from the Gospels, *Christ and the Woman Taken in Adultery* (Philadelphia, Museum of Art) generally considered to be a copy of a lost picture.

Even in paintings more openly religious, like the Philadelphia *Epiphany* which can be considered in relation to the work of the same name in the Prado, or the Brussels *Crucifixion* (1480–85, Musées Royaux des Beaux-Arts), there is no lack of symbolism. The Christ on the cross, between the Madonna and Saint John on the left, and a donor and St Peter on the right, has reminded some scholars, especially by a certain angularity of the bodies, of the *Crucifixion* in the Cathedral of 's-Hertogenbosch, attributed to

Ecce Homo
Museum of Fine Arts, Boston

Christ among the Doctors
Museum of Art, Philadelphia

Ecce Homo p. 61
Staedelsches Kunstinstitut, Frankfurt am Main

Bosch's paternal grandfather Jan van Aken, and in fact the Brussels painting keeps a balance between archaic echoes, the statuesque arrangement of the draperies and the broad vista of the landscape. In the background, in a step-like arrangement between glades and hills, are outlined the monumental buildings of a city: 's-Hertogenbosch? But here and there we can discern more mysterious details: for example the crow on the left, which, to the mystics, means unbelief, and in the language of alchemy the "*nigredo*", that is, the first process of the "*opus magnum*"; while on the right the hollow tree, a symbol of death, also recalls the crucible; and the deep hollow refers to the attempt to penerate the secrets of nature.

Rarefied but meaningful symbolic figures appear also in *Ecce Homo* (1480–85, Frankfurt, Staedtisches Kunstinstitut) of which there is a simpler version in Boston (Museum of Art) perhaps by a workshop. The Frankfurt painting could be related to *Christ among the Doctors* known today through copies (see the one in the Weinzheimer di Settignano collection, Florence) especially in the characteristic way the by-standers are portrayed.

In *Ecce Homo*, in opposition to the tragic figure of Christ, flanked by the cowardly in-difference of Pilate, the crowd comes to life in the well-moulded but physically graceless figures, and the faces which show in their gestures and their cruel and distorted expressions, the blind bestiality of their minds. On the left, in the empty space, X-rays have shown up the figure of a doner, a mute presence taking part in spirit in the drama of the Redeemer.

The alternatives of good and evil are expressed in fierce contrast, with an effectively simple scenic arrangement which shows the event as though on the edge of a stage, the corner of which juts powerfully forward to accentuate

the effect of depth complicated by the series of levels and the empty spaces on the stage. And here too, besides the struggle between good and evil, magnificently displayed, we find the appeal to the symbols of evil: an owl looks out of the small window of the palace; a halberd shows a crescent shape which reappears on the flag in the background city; a frog has landed on the shield of a bystander; heretical and demoniacal threats seem to prefigure and prolong the consequences of the evil act.

If we want to establish a close connection between Bosch's *Ship of Fools* (Paris, Louvre) and the poem *The Ship of Fools* by Sebastian Brandt, published in 1494, we would have to give a date later than this for the painting. But in reality the theme of the boat with merrymakers was familiar to the painter's contemporaries; the "blue ship", *De Blauwe Scuut*, sung in the first decade of the fifteenth century by the poet Jacob van Oestvoren, appeared in the parade of the Carnival of Brabant, and a Brotherhood was even called after it.

The *Praise of Folly* by Erasmus who, as we have said, studied for three years at 's-Hertogenbosch, has affinities with this motif: "We sailed in search of harbours and shores / and could never come to land / our journeys have no end / because no one knows where to land / and thus we have no rest day or night." Whatever may be, for Bosch, the most stimulating source, Brandt's verses coincide with the course of this little ship "at the mercy of all the pleasures of the senses" as Tolnay says. A little coasting vessel close to shore but without a landing-place, loaded as it is with symbols and admonitions: folly does not belong only to one social class, but all, secular and religious, are in the same boat.

The water is dense and solid-looking, more transparent in the background where a headland juts out, reddish brown like the wood of the boat. The leafy hedge is on an unattainable shore, but the top of the tree which serves as a mast (there are no sails) has had its foliage enriched by later additions.

There are eight people in the boat, another is on the branch of a three-branched tree stuck into the hull, two in the muddy water, and yet another is emerging from the hedge. The faces have strong profiles; those seen full-face are blunt and swollen. The clothes are broken up by folds which sometimes look like paper; the absence of direct natural light makes the light reflected from the threads of the garments give a feeling of restlessness. The boat, though small, seems to contain its mad passengers without danger. The first actors are a Franciscan monk and a nun playing a lute which, like the cherries on the table, is an erotic symbol. These two, like three more of their shipmates, are trying to bite a cake hanging on a string, while in the prow another nun with a jug in her hand, an allusion to her sex, is teasing the man who is holding a water-bottle, which is a phallic symbol, over the side of the boat.

In the stern a man is vomiting, the first diabolical sign of the disintegration of the personality. In the water are two nudes—purification by water? But one seems to be trying to climb over the side of the boat.

Among the leaves a petty thief, holding a knife—a symbol of virility—seems to be trying to cut the cord holding the roasted chicken or swan, beneath the flag with the crescent tied to the trunk of the hazel tree, the tree of bestiality, among the leaves of which grins an owl mask.

But apart from other allusions, the strangest character and perhaps the most indicative is the hunchback perched on the forked tree-trunk: the Fool, the twenty second card of the Major Arcana of the Tarot, which indicates the end of

the game and the highest degree of initiation. There are eight people in the boat, completing the ritual death; the Fool is the ninth person: the sign of new life. He is drinking from a ceremonial cup, he is turning his back on the folly of the others, two horns emerge from his hood, and in his left hand he carries a pole to which is affixed a strange head of a nun or a witch. The shimmering threads of his costume emphasise his restless agility, contrasted with the intense green of the foliage.

Infinite meanings and symbols open to many interpretations thus co-exist in this little vessel which at first seems simply to row slowly to the strains of mediaeval Goliard songs. These strains seem to re-appear, not only in the preliminary sketch in the Louvre, but in other works of Bosch, such as the *Concert in the Egg* known only in copies (see for example the one at Lille, Musée Vicar) or the *Allegory of Pleasures* (Yale, University Art Gallery) which some scholars have even supposed, but without evidence, to be the lower part of *The Ship of Fools*.

In the works of his youth symbolism shows through the imagery, promising a revelation of more complex meanings; but the accent on didacticism, clothed with a vast proliferation of images, makes the great moral allegory of Bosch's first maturity.

The Haywain (Madrid, Prado) is the painter's first great triptych and can be dated between 1485 and 1490 (Tolnay) or about 1500 (Baldass), or at the most a little later, 1500–2 (Cinotti). It is signed at the bottom right of the central panel. There exists a second version (Escorial, Monastery of Saint Laurence) signed at the bottom of the left wing and considered to be a replica made in Bosch's workshop. It was one of the artist's paintings acquired by Philip II (1570); it was then taken to pieces and finally put together again in 1914, and in 1939 hung in the Prado for a while with the Escorial version.

Peopled with a dense and overpowering mass of humanity drawn in small figures like those which had already appeared in preceding works, its details sometimes following the dictates of the late Gothic style and echoes of fifteenth century miniatures, but arranged narratively and spatially in a way that almost always overcomes and resolves the difficulties of composition, the triptych avails itself of new pictorial qualities appearing not only in the wide blue space of the background, but also in the use of pure fluid colour, perfectly coinciding with the form. The painter resolves his space vertically in gradual steps from the bottom upwards, with raised horizons above which the clear sky is constantly obstructed by clouds or other elements that seem to echo in heaven the events taking place on earth. The movement which seems to pervade the whole painting with the wings open comes not so much from the sweep of the broad lines of action, as from the ant-like agitation and inexhaustible vitality of every figure, each one faithfully carrying out the role assigned to it.

Bosch's language, though its didactic purpose is sometimes almost too transparent, shows in this work an individuality which is unmistakeable, though later widely imitated or even copied.

All the triptych, a "spectacle of the world", celebrates human folly, and is not deaf to the admonitions of the fourteenth and fifteenth century mystics. The left wing shows the creation of Eve and the banishment from Eden, a tragic premise to the sinful folly of man in the centre, leading to eternal torment on the right. With the wings closed the triptych shows a composition painted continuously over the two panels: the mad pilgrim following the road of sin. This is one of the themes most consonant with Bosch's moral and symbolic attitude; he takes up the

Triptych of the Haywain (detail)
Monastery of St Lawrence, Escorial

Triptych of the Haywain pp. 70-71
Monastery of St Lawrence, Escorial

Triptych of the Haywain (detail)
Monastery of St Lawrence, Escorial

motif again in one of the most difficult works of his late maturity, the Rotterdam *Prodigal Son*.

The landscape helps to give the idea of an inescapable journey: the obliquity of the path, the round-topped hills, the countryside dappled in shades of yellow and green. He is the typical wanderer, or the "son of Saturn", or, for occult science, the Fool, the twenty-second card of the Major Arcana of the Tarot, the final degree of initiation, as witness also the partial uncovering of the knee, and thus the "wandering fool"; he is in any case the witness and participant of human vicissitudes. His eyes do not know where to look, nor whither to lead his steps, which are approaching a rickety bridge; a dog snarls as he passes, and round him lie macabre human bones with black birds flying over them. Behind him are scenes of cruelty and sin: a robbery on the left, while on the right a couple dance on the grass to the sound of a bagpipe, the symbol of lust. Further away on the hill, a gallows is ready, and a concourse of fools is already crowding round for the sight. The prematurely wrinkled face of the wanderer seems marked by the pain of irresolution and regrets. But the warning and the fear of this picture become the tale told in the open triptych.

The Earthly Paradise in the triptych is a scene of primitive naturalness, already poisoned by sin; in the high perspective of wooded glades, meadows and rocks, there is little room for heaven. But among the orange and green clouds, at a gesture from the Almighty, the rebel angels are falling, turning into monstrous multi-coloured insects. At the bottom, in a meadow stained with red, dominated by a vaguely anthropomorphic rock, the creation of Eve is being enacted like a rite.

Sin is lightly committed by the elegant little figures, fascinated by the half-human tempter; and Adam and Eve, only a little upset, keep all the beauty of body and movement as they are banished by a menacing gesture of the angel, to whom emphasis is lent by the drapery of his heavy red mantle.

In the centre is the haywain: "the world is like a haywain, everyone snatches from it what he can". From this Dutch proverb, or others like it, or from verses from Isaiah or the Psalms symbolising by the hay the transient pleasures of life; or from the allegorical processional figures, customary in Flanders at that time, in which "all sorts of people scrambling for the hay, such as usurers, tax-gatherers, merchants, since earthly gain is like hay" followed the cart; or from the Seventh Major Arcana of the Tarot, which shows a cart pulled by sphinxes or horses and alludes to man's path through life; all sources lead to similar motifs with a universal meaning. In fact, although he is using recurrent folk customs, the image of the cart, which summarises all the vanity of life, is for Bosch an opportunity to lay bare the whole catalogue of human folly.

At the bottom left is a magus in a tall hat, then a lady yielding to the insistence of two gipsy women, then suspected of magic arts, one of whom is reading her hand; then a quack doctor at his table, on which stands a strange flag; then a bagpipe player being seduced by a nun, and then corrupt monks and nuns making merry. Above these characters, on the stage, is the episode isolated more than any other, that of murder, carried out in the chaos in which everyone fights for his own part of the treasure.

It is not without significance that, on the left, potentates, ecclesiastic and civil, display their court, with a train of dignitaries. But this bestial folly finds its expression in ferocious brawls (see for analogies in the composition of the groups the *Battle between Carnival and Lent*, The Hague, Cramer Gallery, copy of a work by Bosch, perhaps contemporary with *The Haywain*).

The people are putting even their own safety at risk; many, in fact, finish under the wheels of the cart, which is pulled by strange beings in which the most aberrant changes are taking place—spectral transformations of human illusions? On top of the cart, rich with golden hay, under the puzzled eyes of Christ in judgement, is the climax of the picture: two couples, one exotic, the other musical, are flanked by an angel with wings like a cloth of gold, and a devil with a peacock's tail, playing a trumpet made up of his own lips and nose.

On one side, an owl, of the same indefinite colour as the demon, sits impassively on a branch and looks on at the scene, and on the other, hung on a pole, perhaps held by the curious man, dangles a jug, the symbol of the devil who emerges from it on the night of the Sabbat.

Demoniacal symbols, human chaos, terrible monstrosities move to the convulsive rhythm of madness; all are involved in the same way, and the condemnation of the mystics and the pre-Reformation climate of hatred against the corrupt clergy find pitiless expression.

Finally all is ended: the punishment has for background red-hot walls and a sky burning its own infected air without damaging the apocalyptic buildings, among which the cylindrical tower is being completed and enlarged still more, so as to contain all the sinners. In hell too the composition is graduated on various planes, but in the progression from left to right of the triptych, from the lost quiet of Eden to the convulsive struggles of humanity, spaces contract and draw together in the infernal city to which colour has already given a terrifying, malevolent aspect. A glutton is swallowed by a monstrous fish with human legs; an envious man is caught and torn to pieces by dogs with forked tails; over the bridge, drawn with architectural precision, someone guilty of the sin of pride is dragged along with a frog-devil sitting on his belly; on the level held up by the arch, a man, transfixed by a lance, is carrying a cup; is he a sacrilegious robber, the rider of death, or perhaps the Knight of Cups of the Tarot? *The Vision of Tundale* also shows a character of this type, as the visionary images of Tundale appear in many other works by Bosch, even in some stylistically close to *The Haywain* triptych, such as *The Death of the Upright Man* and *The Death of the Rebrobate* (both at New York, Wildenstein Gallery), attributed to the artist by Tolnay and considered to be the side panels of a triptych which must have had in the centre at Last Judgment now lost.

Fragmentary triptych of the Last Judgment p. 78
The Death of the Reprobate
Gallery Wildenstein, New York

Triptych of the Flood, The World after the Flood
Musée Boymans van Beuingen, Rotterdam

Triptych of the Flood, The World after the Flood
Musée Boymans van Beuningen, Rotterdam

There are possible solutions everywhere, and almost all equally plausible because they can all be referred to Bosch's complex spiritual and cultural world. In *The Haywain* too, the tragic flag of the Hanged Man is hoisted against the fiery sky of the infernal city.

The problem of dating the *Triptych of Delights* carries with it problems relative to the chronology of other works. It seems, however, permissible to state that though the spatial structure can be compared with that of *The Haywain*, with which it has many analogies relative to the partitioning and the vertical graduation of the scenes, *The Garden of Delights*, within a plan already tried in the previous triptych, has a more complex flow of images, plotting events in space without crowding them convulsively, in a way that suggests a more mature use of previous experience. Experience which, as has already appeared obvious, does not follow a foreseeable development, but involves exploration, and a return to primitive imagery connected with the arcane meanings of symbols.

From the unbridled desire that leads to the pitiless struggle round the wheels of the cart to the utterly pagan catalogue of a garden of ineffable delights, the logic of Bosch's thought begins to work on the harsh conception of intellectual temptation: that of the world of hermits.

In comparing the principal works, then, it is not the uncertainty of dates and documentation that matters, but the artistry that seeks and experiments with new themes, carries as far as possible the intensity of a few motifs, explores familiar and arcane sources, even invents unusual iconographies: symbolism is never far away; the opposition between good and evil always present and strong.

In this field of experience we could place paintings like the altarpiece known as that of *St Julia*, or better, according to Cinotti, *St Liberata* (1500–4, Venice, Doge's Palace) in which, though the central part returns in a sense to the imagery and composition of *The Haywain*, the two side panels are related to the *Hermit* altarpieces; and the *Triptych of the Flood*, perhaps contemporary (Rotterdam, Boymans–van Beuningen Museum), of which the central panel has been lost, and which has, on the outside of each of the two wings, two circles representing the "evil world" and the "world after the flood": on the left, the devil at home and the devil in the country; on the right he who is lost and he who is saved; all done in grisaille, in a monochrome beautifully conceived both in the transitions and in the spectral lunar reflections, so as to emphasise the Biblical structure of the scenes; the one showing the world after the flood expresses especially well the slow laboured breathing of a new humanity.

We can place in the same period and a similar context of attempts to resolve colour in tonal harmony, in the archaism of the little figures and the serpentine movement of spaces and groups, the small panels of *The Visions of Beyond* (Venice, Doge's Palace): *Fall of the Damned, Hell, Earthly Paradise, Ascent into the Empyrean*, the last of which has an extraordinary inventive and pictorial quality, with the great funnel of light which seems to attract the souls like a magnet. This, according to Tolnay, was a conception not far removed from Dante, and at the same time appears to illustrate a phrase from the mystic Ruysbroeck (*Adornment of the Spiritual Marriage*) when he speaks of the irradiation of God, an abyss like "an immense essential light".

It may therefore be plausible that, together with other works, those we have mentioned are

Triptych of the Garden of Delights p. 83
The Creation of the World
Prado, Madrid

Triptych of the Garden of Delights pp. 84-85
Prado, Madrid

the link between *The Haywain* and the stylistic obscurity and didactic symbolism of the later works. In these too, if it were possible to indulge here in a more detailed analysis, there are demoniacal elements, signs of Gnostic doctrines, hints of alchemy; everything, in fact, which in the *Triptych of Delights* (Madrid, Prado) offers an incredible multiplicity of interpretations.

Whether the date of the famous triptych is, as almost everyone agrees, about 1510, or even earlier, 1503-4 (Cinotti), does not alter the relationship between *The Haywain* and *The Garden of Delights*, not only because they are thematically complementary—in one, the temptation of worldly goods, in the other, the temptation of pure sensuality—but in their use of space and in the metallic transparency of the colours: elements already emerging in the first triptych.

Philip II had *The Garden of Delights* in his collection, and it was mentioned in inventories and by Spanish writers: "*una pintura de la variedad del mundo*", "*la lujuria*", "*los deleites terrenales*"; with these distinctive titles the Spaniards attributed to it an obvious moralistic slant, particularly emphasised by Father Sigüença who saw in this work the possibility of acting upon souls almost by sorcery, through this terrifying counterblast.

It is certain, however, that the first reading of the triptych must be with the moralistic and didactic key. On the outer wings is the third day of Creation, floating in a crystal sphere; on the left inner wing is *The Earthly Paradise* in which the creation of Eve summarises and prefigures all the evils of the world; in the centre the representation of the sins and especially those of the flesh; in the right-hand wing the punishment: the so-called *Infernal Concert*.

But if this is the first thread, and certainly the most important, that shows the way through the labyrinth of metaphors, it is joined by other meanings that appear, more or less obviously, in the dense tangle of images, human, zoomorphic, vegetable, mineral, and which, for Combe, are open to interpretation as alchemical symbols.

But if alchemy is the science of man's supreme act of pride, since by it he seeks to oppose the Creator, through a desperately difficult process of decantation and purification, this present and undeniable mass of intellectual sin rises above the carnal sins, though without being dissociated from them, because heretical science is based on the union of the masculine with the feminine principle.

The moralistic substratum remains in the end even for Tolnay who tries the psychoanalytic key and sees in the population of *The Garden of Delights* a humanity that seeks to lose its chains by the affirmation of the rights of the unconscious, for which erotic symbolism and in particular that of the "key of dreams" of the late fifteenth century would provide ample material, enriched or supported by popular beliefs and customs.

But though scholars have expressed a variety of possible interpretations, maintaining or partly modifying the moralistic framework of the complex painting, Fraenger has given a bolder direction to his research. The Triptych, according to him, replies to the demands of the Adamite sect, and hell is thus reserved for those heretics who deviate from the complicated gnosis of the sect, as, besides Eden, the central panel prefigures, in the garden of all delights, the reign of the new Adam, aspiring to reach harmony between nature and the spirit; thus every episode and every gesture reflects the rites practised by the sect, that of the Brothers of the Free Spirit and the whole work was not only commissioned but even suggested to Bosch by the "Grand Master". These too are suppositions, suggestive,

Visions of Beyond p. 86
The Ascent into the Empyrean—The Earthly Paradise—
The Fall of the Damned, Doge's Palace, Venice

but, besides the fact that there is no basic documentation, they are not exhaustive. Only recourse to many keys to the code makes it possible, if not to fix the meanings with certainty, at least to get somewhere near unlocking their close-knit symbolism; thus trying to accomplish critically—even if only partially, since so many elements are today incomprehensible—what Bosch accomplished with his brilliant faculty of reception, assimilation and expression, distilling from it a pictorial language which he communicated to his contemporaries in a less hermetic way than to us.

Undoubtedly, however, to anchor the interpretation of these works essentially to the definite possession of a key capable of deciphering the images, may also come up against the unfair distraction of the artistic qualities, which are never separate from the message to be communicated, but form with it one single pictorial whole.

The subtlety of colours, in the most glittering and resonant tones; the crystalline transparency of the atmosphere; the flashing lights of the skies of hell, the inexhaustible invention of the strange forms, and even a vein of acrobatic delight; the use of the painted surface, and of the space on it, according to a system which not only has a didactic purpose, but does its utmost to make every element contain a peculiar fantastic beauty, touched with a disturbingly exotic feeling; the rarity of a language that feeds on its own qualities and renews them—all unite to give the measure of Bosch's art, before and beyond the exciting problems posed by his vision. A Gothic style, late and uneasy and thus a most sensitive catalyst of all the strange alchemy of the intellect. The whole work—and, even more, a few particular episodes of the central panel—recalls the rhythm of "triumphs"; and even the partial copies that have been made

of it seem to have this highly illustrative and celebratory character.

The closed wings of the triptych present a composition continuing over the two faces; in a crystal sphere the world is undergoing the third day of creation, under a sky thick with clouds, massed towards the top, accentuating the sense of separation. The earth is coagulating and separating from the waters which form a ring round it, while its first germination and birth is slow and wearisome, almost like a dull rumbling, in grisaille varied by browns. Everything in this terrible and solemn panorama seems to be related to the faded, floating world after the flood (see the Rotterdam *Triptych of the Flood*), even the vaguely distinguishable vegetable and mineral forms, all alike in the process of formation.

The Creator, in the top left-hand corner, in an unusual iconography, seems the first spectator rather than the agent; but his work is referred to in the old text, in Gothic characters: "*Ipse dixit et facta su(n)t / Ipse ma(n)davit et creata su(nt).*" "For he spake, and it was done; he commanded, and it stood fast." (Psalms XXXIII, 9). The crystalline sphere of the globe is the forerunner of the constant use of spherical forms and transparent materials shown in the whole of the Triptych, the crucible of a unique form of creation.

In the left wing, *The Earthly Paradise* is a marvellous garden of vegetable, animal and mineral rarities in which everything is condensed into a single episode, the Creation of Eve, the origin and starting-point of the evils of the world, thus omitting all the other episodes belonging to Eden, already shown in *The Haywain*, *The Visions of Beyond* and also in *The Earthly Paradise* (Chicago Art Institute) which, in a way, freely takes up the motifs of the *Triptych of Delights*. Eve is presented to Adam, wakened after his long sleep, by the Creator, who looks like Christ, according to the ancient tradition. For Fraenger the scene could mean the confirmation of sexual union through Christ. But the landscape of Eden, darkened by the stagnant pond in the foreground, concentrated by the clear waters of the Fountain of Life in the centre, and, in the background, diagonally extended by a succession of strange surreal rock formations, is already disturbed by odd episodes and a subtle shiver of fear which alters or exalts the creatures of this uneasy paradise: on the shores of the pond and in its waters are fish, birds, zoomorphic monsters which are already plotting one against another, while a small three-headed dragon is leaping upon a sea-horse, and further left a cat is running away with a mouse in its jaws. Behind the realistic but uncomfortably positioned figure of Adam is a monstrous tree, with a trunk made up of roots to which the leaves are directly attached like sharp-edged feathers. Around the Fountain of Life is a crowd of animals, sometimes exactly reproduced, but more often tending to the exotic and abnormal, very near to the monstrous; and there is no lack of episodes of cruelty and horror. And even the charming monument of the fountain carries a menace: from the circular eye in the spherical base peers that heretical symbol of wisdom, the owl; it is adorned in several places with the diabolical sign of the crescent; while on the right the legendary palm recalls original sin in the serpent twisting about its trunk.

Spirals of birds are emerging from the hollow in the first gilded rock, and perhaps others are sheltering in the monstrous shapes which are both vegetable and mineral and provoke that shudder of dread which is already evident in other works by Bosch. At the foot of the first rock a stone egg is the refuge of crows, the symbol of unbelief for the mystics, but also an alchemic allusion to the "nigredo", the first stage of the "opus".

Evil has already entered Eden: the first appearance scarcely hides the poison of sin; its seed is already in the fields that shiver under the first magic spells.

And as man's cupidity struggled blindly to the death under the wheels of *The Haywain*, *The Garden of Delights* shows in its central panel all the temptations of the senses; it is "neglect of one's neighbour in glorifying pure sensation" (Castelli). The nude, therefore, triumphs in all its possible forms: rosy, tender nudes, often side by side with black nudes, in the strangest positions, but always traceable to an erotic meaning set off by groupings and episodes, by the symbolism of ornament, by their closeness to unusual plant forms, separated in recesses carefully calculated on the sunlit surface, shown on horseback and bathing, in evil and exhausting embraces, and near the monstrous spherical monuments, almost like a foretaste of science fiction, which stand in a semi-circle in the background.

Every image, treated like a miniature rather than a painting, stands out in the neat strong profiles and the intelligent, meaningful elegance of the gestures, rendered more obvious by the delicate beauty of the limbs; rosy or sometimes black, they are set against colours which correspond symbolically to the painter's intentions: blue, which in all its darker shades means deceit, orange which indicates a stage of the alchemical process, in which red signifies the conclusive moment. The sense of movement comes not so much from the dynamics of separate figures as from the unrestrained clustering and flowing of the nudes in predominantly diagonal and circular directions, so as to give the idea of a multiplication of space in the

Triptych of the Garden of Delights
The Garden of Delights (detail)
Prado, Madrid

Triptych of the Garden of Delights
The Garden of Delights (detail)
Prado, Madrid

multiplicity of the actions taking place in it.

It is very difficult to explain logically the labyrinth of delights which for Tolnay has some echoes of the *Apocalypse* of Baruch; for Combe on the other hand it is to be understood, with some probability, as woven of the dreams of minds lulled to sleep by sin; for Fraenger it is nothing but the return to an innocent *ars amatoria* commended by the Adamites.

It is in any case certain that the *Garden* is the triumph of erotic excitement, contemplated in all its aspects and events, with an artist's joy which seems very often to blur his moralistic intentions.

Very many suggestions are contained in the picture, with the same incredible facility with which the most unimaginable monstrosities abound—the mystics' esoteric temptations and fertility of images, popular beliefs and heretical science. Everything Bosch does corresponds entirely to the composite, many-facetted quality of his culture. In virtue of this, and of those glimpses of light already seen in other pictures, we can try to extract some key points. For example, the single clothed figure in this paradise of nudes, who is emerging from the ground in the far right-hand corner: a man, with a male head behind him, who is pointing to a woman with her lips sealed: is it meant to be original sin (Tolnay), or the painter, the Grand Master of the Adamites who commissioned it, and Eve (Fraenger), or Noah, Adam and Eve (Bax)? Again it is an unsolvable mystery, but it is certain that the seal on the woman's mouth and the great glass phial through which she is seen, allude to an esoteric secret and to alchemy.

Glass cylinders, spheres and phials constantly recur in the painting, always symbolising hermetic science, as does also the presence of flowers, fruit and animals, always clearly symbolic. On this subject, the focal point is marked by the geometric centre of the painting, that is, the egg which a knight in the centre is carrying on his head; the egg and egg-shapes indicate the alembic of the alchemists, and so constitute a diabolical emblem.

Winged beings fly or ride in the sky, perhaps freed from the monstrous vegetable and mineral machines of exquisite colouring, the refuge of lovers and birds, in groups showing phallic and sexual symbols side by side with heretical ones, among which that of the crescent is repeated many times.

In the pond of blue, calm, deceptive water, there are innumerable erotic games, especially in and around the so-called Fountain of Adultery, while a throng of men, on the left, lands on the alchemical egg.

Birds and marine monsters blend their rare hues with those of the rock and coral concretions, and the huge flowers and fruits, while in the circular Fountain of Youth—for which Bosch must have had recourse not only to visual impressions gained from miniatures, but perhaps rather to mediaeval customs—women are bathing in the illusion of incorruptible youth, not caring that around them or over their heads hover the crows of unbelief, the ibises that recall past joys, or the peacocks of vanity. The dream of a life of joy and oblivion, which has its elixir in the fountain, is glorified in the triumphal procession: goats, panthers, camels, stags, unicorns, wild boars, horses, in a fabulous exotic medley, carry frenzied riders in a circular motion that has no end, and seems, in fact, to be attracting fresh adepts.

And there are other delights too: on the right in an enchanted garden of forbidden fruits; on the left in waters peopled by birds of immense size, signifying a warning: the owl, with its meaning of heresy and alchemy, the wild duck, the kingfisher, the woodpecker, which have a magic significance, the robin, symbol of lust. The source of the ancient bestiaries is enriched with implications and hidden meanings; and despite the disproportionate appearance, direct observation makes the images more exact and realistic. Every element of this all-pervasive, abnormal nature has gigantic proportions which emphasise the symbolism in their apparent illogicality: the fish, a phallic symbol or a memory of past pleasures; the great mussel, a female symbol, containing two lovers and carried by a man, perhaps a deceived husband. In the pool, among the other bathers, a man plunging head-first carries between his parted legs a fruit which is opening like an egg, letting out a little stork. Next to him, one of the mysterious figures: an enigmatic couple in an air-bubble breathed out by a thistle-flower, the symbol of temptation, and supported by an enormous fruit which a mouse, the symbol of falsity, enters through a glass tube.

Berries and fruit of every size are the object of infinite pansexual play, the symbol of unbridled sensuality and perhaps also an allusion to the power of drugs and hallucinating foods. And there is the transparency of the little bells of air, crystal or fruit, and the coral solidity of forms like the inverted Y-shape or little tower in whose not very discreet shelter androgyny is being practised. The signs and symbols are piled one upon the other without taking anything away and without troubling the whirling flow of the picture.

Mysterious acrobatics and black rituals are going on in *The Infernal Concert*. Here too there is a focal point like the sphere with the eye in which an owl shelters in Eden, and the egg on the rider's head in the Garden; but the central nucleus of hell can also be understood as the focal point of the whole painting, which would confirm Fraenger's hypothesis that the Triptych

should be read from right to left: it is *The Alchemical Man*, the monstrous being, pervaded with the colours of alchemy, blue, white, red. His feet, like trees or pig's trotters, are supported on boats, for Tolnay the "blue boat" of destruction. His body is a jaggedly broken egg, very like a hollow tree, sheltering an infernal tavern, which a man is trying to enter by climbing a ladder, and is transfixed from behind by an arrow symbolising pederasty, while he carries a jug, the sign of the devil, suspended from a pole. The human head of the monster (a self-portrait?) a mirror of all knowledge, is motionless, weighed down by the millstone which symbolises the obsessional pressure of his thoughts, and on which, as an emblem, stands the sexual symbol of the red bagpipes, around which diabolical pantomimes are going on.

But around the stillness of the mute watcher every movement is convulsive: in the sky and in the burning city invaded by rioting hordes and dense throngs of riders, instruments of torture, daring rope-walkers, hanged men. Two enormous ears, symbols of unhappiness, transfixed by a phallic knife-blade, are sweeping away the damned; another blade is a terrible instrument of torture for creatures menaced by fearful dogs. Step by step, as the journey of damnation moves dismally to the foreground, the engines of torture become sinister musical instruments whose uproar, the negation of harmony, appears to be trying to cover howls and lamentations.

Seated on a high chair a monstrous demon with a bird's head is devouring men from whom the crows of heresy are escaping, and is excreting them into a green glass ball, letting them fall into a sewer, around which one man is excreting gold coins while another is vomiting, the first demoniacal warning of the disintegration of the personality.

The whole infinite catalogue of fantastic

Triptych of the Last Judgment, Vienna p. 96
St Bavo
Akademie der Bildenden Künste, Vienna

Triptych of the Last Judgment, Vienna
St James of Compostela
Akademie der Bildenden Künste, Vienna p. 96

Triptych of the Last Judgment, Vienna
Akademie der Bildenden Künste, Vienna

punishments cannot be restricted to these few examples; every moment has its unrepeatable horror, up to the episode in the far corner on the right, showing a pact with the devil, in which a man, urged on by a horrible monster with legs attached directly to its helmet, is being lasciviously tempted by a sow wearing a nun's veil, and is assisted by a man who bears on his head tablets with alchemical texts, and wears embroidered on his robe the Satanic spell of the toad.

The range of horrors is so vast that it cannot be compared with any other pictorial imagery, though according to Tolnay it is related to Dante and may also have links with the horrible images of the *Visio Tundali* and those of the *Grand Calendrier des Bergers* (1493).

Orthodoxy and heterodoxy, mysterious gnoses and arcane sciences lend material for the imagery and can at least partially help to decipher the meaning of the spells and the episodes. The theatre of events is the frozen pond which, for Castelli, is "the inevitable end of pure sensation".

The forerunner of *The Alchemical Man* is to be found particularly in the drawing of *The Tree-man* in the Albertine Gallery, which, apart from a few variants, corresponds to the monstrous being in the Triptych, in its attributes and symbols.

Carnal sin is especially represented in it, but, as in all the other motifs of the painting, it is also the mirror of a soul tossed and torn by unbelief, heresy and false doctrines; as in a witches' cauldron, the misery of mankind has here its negative triumph, in a hallucinatory tension which captures the mind, spreading through space and time, a distant but irrefutable reference to *The Garden of Delights* and *The Infernal Concert*.

One particular problem has interested scholars —that of the letter M incised on the two gigantic blades which appear in hell. It was interpreted at first as the signature of Jan Mandyn or Jan Mostaert, or supposed to be the initial of a cutler of s'-Hertogenbosch, placed among the sinners detested by the artist. Tolnay suggests the hypothesis that it alludes to *Mundus*, a sign of universality, which can be assimilated to the male symbol, while Combe sees in it the zodiacal sign of Scorpio, with reference to sulphur, the male element of the alchemists.

But these menacing signed knives appear in two more works which most scholars consider to be mainly by Bosch's workshop, with a few additions by Bosch himself; they are the *Triptych of the Last Judgment* in Vienna (Kunstakademie) and the *Triptych of the Last Judgment* in Bruges (Groeninge Museum) which use, though sometimes without much conviction, the fantastic imagery of *The Infernal Concert*, from the diabolical instruments of torture to the "grilli" or "freaks"—that is to say the hybrid monsters with lower limbs attached to deformed heads, images very frequent in Bosch's pictorial world, far from the delicate and elaborate *drôleries* of French miniatures, and more closely related to the "pygmy" of the Greek or Hellenistic type, the exaggeration of all those grotesque figures derived from the name of Ulysses' companion Grillo, who, turned into a pig by Circe, refused to be turned back into a man.

In any case Bosch's final secret lies in the letter M incised on the blade of cruel knives, even if circumstances, and more still the analysis of the images among which it is found, appear to support the hypothesis of a large contribution by collaborators and assistants.

In these *Last Judgment* triptychs, even the inevitable panel of *The Earthly Paradise* derives, more or less conventionally, from the scheme of *The Garden of Delights*, the language of which, largely purified of the disturbing atmosphere and lifted into a delicate and distant landscape, gleaming with crystalline light, forms the broad vision of *St John on Patmos* (1504–5, Berlin–Dahlem, Ehemals Staatliche Museum) and the contemporary *St John the Baptist in Meditation* (Madrid, Lázaro Galdiano Museum) in which, however, nature is pervaded by a fantastic luxuriance, again full of symbols and warnings.

Quantitatively less crowded, but qualitatively consistent and meaningful, are the warnings and symbols appearing in pictures which iconographically correspond to the traditional themes of the engravings and miniatures, not to mention the versions of the Golden Legend: *St Christopher* (1504–5, Rotterdam, Boymans van Beuningen Museum) carries the Christ Child on his shoulders; he bears "the burden of the world", and leans firmly upon a stick, with his feet in the transparent water, gigantic against the wide landscape that stretches into a moist

infinity in a misty sweetness of colour. The other episodes in the painting are clear, but at the same time lost in the expanse of nature; on the distant shore the naked man threatened by a dragon alludes to the past history of the giant, who abandoned the devil to devote himself to the service of God; a peasant hangs up a bear he has killed in the chase, while a hermit holds up a large fish with his stick, "the fast that follows the conversion and Lent". A jug, sign of the devil, hollow like the body of the Alchemical Man, and reached only by a ladder, is placed in a forked tree, at the top of which the bee-hive and the dove-cot allude to the temptations of the senses.

Still more subtle are the manifestations of evil in the *Little St Christopher* of Madrid (private collection) with the little army having a flag with the crescent as its standard; and finally more obvious in the *Winterthur St Christopher*

(Reinhart collection), where they dispute the ford leading to salvation. Each of these works bears the seeds of the *Hermit* paintings, in which Bosch aims to reveal the temptation of the intellect in the denunciation of the devil's wiles. They are not scenes from hell in the sense of eternal punishment for sin, but visions of the Sabbat in which is acted out the perpetual struggle between contemptation and temptation, between God and the devil.

The *Altarpiece of the Hermits* (Venice, Doge's Palace) can be dated around 1505, and perhaps slightly precedes the Lisbon Triptych. St Anthony in the left-hand panel, St Jerome in the centre and St Giles on the right, indicate three paths of internal struggle and salvation, three ways to mystical exaltation in their spiritual steps, as Ruysbroeck says in *The Book of the Highest Truth*.

Despite the fact that the state of preservation of the picture is not of the best, and the colours are darkened, in certain parts we are aware of the search for tonal effects and the intention to extend and set out the landscape in such a way as to include the stories of the hermits and the symbolic references.

In the panel with St Anthony, in the background of which the burning city seems to allude to the Saint's power over fire and, according to popular belief, over all skin diseases, there are freaks, monsters and demons; one mockingly reads a missal, another spins the peacock's tail round, and another, shaped like a fish, dabbles the jug, symbol of the devil, in the pond. There is no lack of alchemical references, given with mischievous pastoral elegance: the naked woman, like a queen according to the hagiographical text, is maliciously revealed by the mantle raised by a man accompanying her and bathes in the accursed water: this is a female, thus a diabolical element, attempting the

heretical union of fire and water.

No less alluring are the complex temptations of St Jerome who, discarding his cardinal's hat and abandoned by the lion, gesticulates in front of the crucifix placed in a ruined pagan altar shaped like a throne, while behind him an idol falls from its complicated pedestal which bears a sunworshipper in bas-relief, and, lower down, shows an owl looking through a circular hole. There are erotic and alchemical symbols at his feet and behind his back, culminating in the hut with its roof of monstrously luxuriant plant life. The marble bas-reliefs refer to the possibility of redemption: the rider trying to bestride a unicorn, symbol of chastity, or the episode of Judith and Holofernes; but on the sloping support of the throne, a man is head down in a bee-hive, gorging himself on honey, that is, on all the delights of the senses.

On the other panel, St Giles is interceding for the souls of those whose names are written on the scroll deposited there, according to the Golden Legend, by an angel. There are few symbols: in the foreground is a small hollow tree and an evil toad, and in the background a flight of birds, perhaps crows.

Similar motifs, with others more unusual, recur in the "hermit" panels of the *Triptych of the Patience of Job* (Bruges, Groeninge Museum), which is, however, of doubtful authorship. But all of them, with a depth of contemplation which goes above and beyond the slow encumbrance of didactic purpose, combine the conceptual with the pictorial, and so lead to the visionary exaltation of the *Triptych of the Temptations of St Anthony* at Lisbon (1505–6, Museu Nacional de Arte Antiga). This, as Castelli remarks, completes the third period of demoniacal temptation: after the temptation of earthly goods (*Haywain*) and that of pure sensuousness (*Garden of Delights*) comes "intellectual temptation through

laceration by the incomprehensibility of the horrible": seduction is replaced by torture, and in the will to resist and not flee is the possibility of salvation.

The theme, which corresponds perfectly to the pre-Reformation demands of northern Europe, to the warnings of the mystics, full of fantastic images, to the *Malleus Maleficarum*, not to mention the Papal Bull "*Summis desiderantes affectibus*" (1484), hurled against the "*sectam maleficorum*", in which the description of magic spells is more exciting than their condemnation, was often taken up by Bosch in other dimensions and with different forms; and it must have been an eloquent stimulus to horrific meditations, since there are about fifteen copies of the Lisbon Triptych alone.

However, apart from this, what confirms the strength of the artist's language is the intrinsic pictorial quality with its varied use of light and shade. He contracts the space allotted to the main events by oblique vectors, resolving the terraced effect of previous triptychs into narrative centres mainly embedded in solidly delineated structures, and prolonging the vision in a continual proliferation of information and warnings, beyond the background which is framed by angular diagonals, as far as the sky crossed by demoniacal processions, typifying the instinct of the human race for pride and seduction; while the undulating, arched elegance of the late Gothic style adds delicacy to the elongated beauty of the images, to which these movements give a three-dimensional quality, full and perfect.

But though the triptych opens upon the most orgiastic vision expressed by Bosch, the closed wings, in grisaille, carry scenes arranged in an arc shape, probably the remains of a more obviously architectural frame.

On the left wing the arrest of Christ takes place in a pale, lurid setting. In the foreground Peter strikes at Malchus, Judas flees with the reward for his betrayal, and on the rocky mountain appears the cup of sacrifice.

On the right wing, the good thief is ensuring the salvation of his soul, while the bad thief, his eyes bandaged, is refusing salvation. In the centre Christ meets Veronica, who is kneeling and leaning forward in a dramatic attitude. It is a moment of great suspense, a breathing-space amid the ill-will of the crowd, a show enjoyed by the indifferent and well-fed citizen who has brought his children with him.

The tumultuous catalogue of the temptations suffered by St Anthony came to Bosch from the life of the Saint written by St Anastasius in 375, two years after the hermit's death, and from the *Golden Legend* of Jacobus de Voragine, which is full of hagiographical ideas for the "innumerable temptations of the demons".

Even if, following Puyvelde's thesis, we chose to see in the fantastic proliferation of monsters and illogicalities, not temptations but torments inflicted by devils on the hermit, unshakeable in his faith, it would not entitle us to ignore the quantity of erotic and alchemical symbols which every image contains, and which scholars have tried to decipher according to the keys and sources which form the substratum of Bosch's world.

The left-hand panel is presented with a complexity of composition which is both bold and measured, not only in the rhythm of the action but in the disposition of space from the foreground to the sea; every scenic possibility is exploited by the zig-zag arrangement of the planes until the sky too is involved. There—while in the middle of the deceptively quiet bay a ship is sinking, with an allusion to the shipwreck of

108

Triptych of the Temptations p. 110
Meditation of St Anthony (detail)
Museu Nacional de Arte Antiga, Lisbon

Temptation of St Anthony
Gallery of Art, Kansas City

the soul—we see Anthony's miraculous flight. Carried off by devils at dizzy speed, or perhaps dragged towards a terrifying and mysterious vision, he holds his body thrown back, his face looking upwards, his hands joined in the prayer of extremity.

The flight is horrifying escortedly by a throng of monsters, fish (memories of past pleasures or phallic symbols) and a little ship with a broken mast and a strange crew which may also be an allusion to the Zodiac.

The landscape is no less pregnant with symbols; the hut is transformed into an obscene shelter by the man whose backside forms the entrance, while his head, thrust out at the other side, is transfixed, a symbol of self-destruction. A sacrilegious procession is walking to the hermitage, while a monster with bagpipes is watching the group of men crossing the bridge. Anthony, who has crashed to the earth after his flight, is helped and urged forward by his fellow-monks; there are two, and the third man, according to St Athanasius's text, is a layman. Is it a self-portrait of the artist? It is probable, and Fraenger notes the bare knee as an element of initiation, inclined as he always is to consider Bosch to be involved in a mysterious gnostic group.

But on the water, the icy crust of which is scarcely broken, skates a monster with a cruel beak, carrying an obscure message—an allusion, according to Combe, to the trade in indulgences —directed to the vulgar figure of the ecclesiastic who is reading, or pretending to, assisted by two demons.

On the left is the alchemical form of the open egg on which a great bird is devouring its new-born young: an anti-pelican and thus a symbol of Antichrist?

But the most impressive thing is the mortal physical weariness of the group, the incurable

Temptation of St Anthony p. 112
Prado, Madrid

Temptation of St Anthony p. 113
Staatliche Museen, Berlin

The Adoration of the Magi
Metropolitan Museum, New York

heaviness contrasted with the restless swarm of the witches' Sabbat. Despite the help, the Saint shows clearly the abyss of his solitude. This is his temptation and also his possibility of salvation.

In the central panel, where the throng at its most furious converges upon him, Anthony stands out, looking at the observer and blessing as though in a last attempt at a comforting human contact, while in the depths of the chapel Christ appears, pointing at the Crucifix. The sky is still infested with flying devils, the city burns without ceasing, while the diabolical hordes come slowly nearer to the Saint, and gradually, as the groups appear to reach the scene of the hermit's arduous meditation, the devilish apparitions become more alluring, and take on more convincing forms. In fact, while a devil-priest celebrates the Black Mass at the foot of the tower, behind the Saint's back the sacrilegious Eucharist is taking place; a prince (perhaps the Antichrist?) is offering the drink to a character (according to Castelli a priest of Baal) with a pig's head surmounted by an owl, a lute under his arm, assisted by a hunchbacked buffoon (the Fool of the Tarot?). Behind the dignitary is a devil-creature whose trumpet, formed directly from his beak, is emitting poisonous vapour; but the women surrounding him, priestesses, conform to conventional ideas of beauty; the plump negress, symbol of heresy, carries on a dish the frog of sorcery which holds aloft an egg; a sacrilegious allusion to the Host or a symbol of the alchemist's crucible; finally a diaphonous priestess, dressed in the Oriental style, and an elegant Brabantine lady offering a dish to the old nun, beside whom there is a monster with a head which may well be a self-portrait of Bosch. At the bottom left a magus in a high-crowned hat appears from a kind of theatrical box; he has in front of him, lying on a

The Kleinberger Johnson Adoration
The Procession of the Magi
Museum of Art, Philadelphia

The Kleinberger Johnson Adoration
Adoration of the Shepherds
Museum of Art, Philadelphia

The Kleinberger Johnson Adoration
The Procession of the Magi
Museum of Art, Philadelphia

The Kleinberger Johnson Adoration
Adoration of the Shepherds
Museum of Art, Philadelphia

115

cloth, a severed foot, an alchemical symbol referring to the fixation of mercury. Is the magus perhaps the producer of the whole display? Behind him, from a red pumpkin which also refers to the alchemist's crucible, emerge diabolical monsters, one of whom is plucking the strings of a psaltery.

Other demons burst in from the left, rowing on the frozen water, while on the left advances a vile cavalcade intended perhaps to parody that of the Magi or the flight into Egypt. They are nightmare images: the first rider, with the head of a thistle (a flower that means temptation for whoever dreams of riches got without effort) bestrides a steed in the shape of a jug, the sign of the devil; his followers are no less ambiguous, and, above all, the woman riding a rat (false doctrine) who looks like a pale hollow tree (the crucible) and holds in her arms the alchemical baby.

The impious allusions form a kind of symphony of temptation, up to the gallery with nudes, which dominates a stagnant pond and forms a bridge to a building the egg-shape of which once more recalls the symbols of alchemy.

The hermit is alone and motionless, remaining rigidly apart from the diabolical rhythm. Even the semi-cylindrical tower appears to be falling into ruins; its bas-reliefs perhaps relate the story of a Biblical salvation.

In the third panel the rhythm of the meditation is slower and the landscape wider; only one demon couple, carrying a jug, ride a fish through the sky. Below is a fabulous Oriental city with sunlit buildings, and a windmill moves its sails through the air.

Lust and gluttony tempt the hermit, with insidious, disturbing intellectual implications. At the bottom is a table laid for a diabolical feast, held up by demons, one of whom has his foot in a jug; on it stands an alembic with a

Triptych of the Epiphany
Prado, Madrid

Triptych of the Epiphany p. 119
Adoration of the Magi (detail)
Prado, Madrid

Triptych of the Epiphany p. 120
Adoration of the Magi (detail)
Prado, Madrid

Triptych of the Epiphany p. 121
St Peter and the Donor (detail)
Prado, Madrid

Triptych of the Epiphany
Adoration of the Magi (detail)
Prado, Madrid

magical pig's trotter stuck into it; a toad leaps from the table on which are bread, flowers, herbs—allusions to foods with secret powers?

The tempting image of the bather which we have already seen in the *Altarpiece of the Hermits* now returns, emerging naked from the hollow tree, the mantle above her lifted off by an enormous toad for whom an old woman pours an evil drink. A hideous monster is at the Saint's feet, with a knife stuck in its belly, and a red hood which leaves an ear uncovered, the organ which receives only the worst stimuli. But more horrible still is the senile child moving with difficulty in the walking frame behind the hermit, the evil offspring of the tree-woman, that is, of alchemist's trickery, fruit of diabolical science and breeding against nature, a symbol of the supreme temptation which in the appearance of infancy and senility, brings together in itself the beginning and the end.

In the other paintings which use the hermit theme and bring together the temptation motifs, in an atmosphere which to some extent remains in touch with reality (see the *Temptations of St Anthony*, Kansas City, Gallery of Art), or imitates it in a sort of orgiastic anti-nature, the dream-world is glorified and the diabolical motifs and proliferation of monsters exaggerated, as in the *Temptation of St Anthony* of 's-Hertogenbosch (Central Nordbrabants Museum), in the painting of the same name at Haarlem (Gutman collection), in that of Brussels (Van Buuren collection), the authorship of which is still controversial, as it is for that of Berlin (Ehemals Staatliche Museum). But although in these paintings the multiplication of elements often loses its force of concentration, the same fantastic vitality, supported by clarity of style and the desire to construct every image with energy, so that every group is like a whirlpool against the reddish brown background, re-

appears intact in the Munich *Last Judgment* (1505–6, Alte Pinakothek), a fragment of the Judgment commissioned in 1504 by Philip the Handsome.

Still keeping to these themes, the Madrid *Temptations of St Anthony* (1510, Prado) brings in a wider vision, a quieter, more inward feeling, in which the temptations partly lose their obvious virulence, tamed, as it were, by the calm, hermit-like aura of the landscape. The Saint, accompanied by the pig, with the Tau-cross of the Antonine order on his habit, according to Bosch's custom, while another Tau-cross surmounts the lych-gate of the chapel, is received into the hollow tree, which seems purified of all evil, unless, as Se Solier says, we should see, in the opposition of the tree and the stream, the alternative between that temptation and the mystic thirst.

Devils and monsters, armed with jugs and knives, roam around the countryside, but like the horrible creature that is pretending to drown, they do not disturb the Saint in his meditation; he seems to represent the hermitage of Ruysbroeck in the forest of Groenandel. Nature rediscovers its peaceful harmony, while Anthony, in the words of the mystic, sees "the things that are beyond all knowledge".

The smaller number of symbols, the poetic softening of all didactic vehemence, the warm sunlit beauty of the landscape in its clear intense colouring, and yet the new and intimately moulded solidity of the figures, make this painting chronologically and also qualitatively close to Bosch's last great triptych, the Madrid *Epiphany* (1510, Prado).

This theme, with its sober but solid reference to Biblical images, had already occupied Bosch in his youth (see the *Epiphany*, 1480–85, Philadelphia Musum of Art) and it recurs in pictures roughly contemporary with the Madrid one, but

Christ Crowned with Thorns
Monastery of St Lawrence, Escorial

Head of a Halberdier
Prado, Madrid

whose authenticity is sometimes rejected or questioned by scholars, like the *Triptych of the Epiphany* (Anderlecht, Brussels, Church of SS Peter and Guy), the New York *Adoration of the Magi* (Metropolitan Museum) or the *Kleinberger-Johnson Adoration*, made up of a central panel (New York, Kleinberger Galleries) and fragments of the two side panels, with the *Adoration of the Shepherds* and the *Procession of the Magi*, both at Philadelphia (Museum of Art, Johnson collection). The new sculptural solidity of the figures and the broad harmony of the landscape —no longer disturbed by visionary temptations, and abominable nightmares, but rose and gold in the calm light of Holland, in which a few shaggy monsters difficult to explain still find a place—take nothing away, but rather confirm first impressions as iconographically correct.

In the Madrid *Epiphany* the draperies fall in solid, naturalistic folds, suggesting the mature

bodies beneath them, very different from the fleshless nudes in *The Garden of Delights*; and they are set off by spatial arrangements which appear simplified, but are in reality composed with extraordinary accuracy; all these elements appear, too, as though filtered through the formal, subtle and persuasive manner of van Eyck or the Master of Flémalle. Although the figurative and iconographical theme is far from unique and isolated in Bosch's work, in the Prado painting it reaches a stylistic coherence which involves every part of the triptych and seems to reply (according to Tolnay, Combe and Delevoy) to a wish to illustrate the sacrifice of the Mass, rather than express the struggle between Christ and Antichrist, as Brand-Philip thinks, even if we do not take into account the fact that Bosch's fellow-adherents of the cult of Our Lady interpreted the *Epiphany* as an image of their devotion to the Madonna, tending to identify themselves with the Magi.

The picture may therefore be considered also in this devotional context. Donated by the Broncklorst and Bosschuyse families to the chapel of the Brotherhood, or the Chapel of the Holy Mother in the Cathedral of 's-Hertogenbosch, it escaped the wave of inconoclasm in August 1566 and was subsequently confiscated (1568) by the Duke of Alba from Jan van Casembroot who had taken it to Brussels. It was then sent as a gift to Philip II who had it transferred to the Escorial (1574). If this is the same painting that Father Sigüença described as "without any eccentricity", the remark appears to fit in with the first glance at the picture, which, with the wings closed, shows in grisaille *The Mass of St Gregory*.

The Saint is shown in the fervour of prayer, at the foot of the altar which is dominated by Christ rising from the coffin, and framed by one cornice of angels in various positions, and then

another cornice with scenes of the Passion culminating in the crucifixion, the chiaroscuro of
which gives them such an effect of relief that
they leap into life with an eloquence of their
own, as though every event could happen again
at Gregory's prayer. All the bystanders are in
grisaille, except the layman on the left, in a
greenish-black robe, perhaps the donor's dead
father, and the small figure that stands out in a
red hood contrasting with the black cloak, which
Tolnay says is maybe the Roman woman who
did not believe in transubstantiation. This
important representation of the Mass, firmly
constructed in its lines of perspective, opens to
show the *Epiphany* flanked by two panels show-

ing on the left St Peter and the donor, Peter
Bronckhorst, and on the right St Agnes and the
other donor, Agnes Bosschuyse.

Though the central panel reminds us of the
Master of Flémalle in the Dijon *Adoration of the
Shepherds*, and the pose of the Madonna with
the Child and the devotional solemnity of the
gesture and the drapery resemble the *Madonna
of Chancellor Robin* by Jan van Eyck, in Bosch's
painting every element is preparing to assume
hitherto unknown meanings.

The Madonna shows the Child like the Host
in the monstrance, and presents him to be
adored. The story urges on to its climax: the
procession of the Magi, usually shown, is here

The Prodigal Son
Musée Boymans van Beuningen, Rotterdam

The Prodigal Son (detail) *p. 129*
Musée Boymans van Beuningen, Rotterdam

of Sheba to King Solomon, prefiguring the journey of the Magi; on the border is the sacrifice of Manoah and the annunciation of the birth of John the Baptist, Christ's precursor. The Moorish king, dressed in a splendid white robe adorned at neck and sleeves with raised embroidery of acanthus leaves, and on the tunic hem with winged monsters, carries in his hand the ciborium of myrrh on which is embossed the episode of the three heroes offering water to David, another prefiguration of the journey of the Magi, surmounted by a bird (a hawk or a pelican?) pecking a fruit; the jewelled strawberry which Caspar holds in his hand is a symbol of heresy.

But the representation becomes more complex in the identification of the other bystanders.

A strange figure stands on the threshold of the hut, and seems not to dare to advance: he is half-naked, a leg and a shoulder protrude, perhaps as a symbol of initiation, from his red cloak; below the calf a wound is seen through a transparent bandage, on his arm he has a gold chain, perhaps a sign of slavery; he is crowned with thorns, but an exquisite tiara hangs from his left hand. Is he a representation of the Jewish Messiah? That is Tolnay's hypothesis; but this figure could also suggest Antichrist or an allegorical image of heresy spying on believers, as Combe thinks. However, his glance seems not to be fixed on the event but on something outside the observer's field of vision.

But against the sumptuous picture of the kings there are other reasons for perplexity. The bad shepherds are moved by malicious curiosity; one is climbing a tree, hoping to see better, one is peeping through a crack in the hut, and one is sitting on the thatched roof: one of the two has a large knife stuck in his cap, and the other, pale and emaciated, is steadying himself by leaning on a deflated bagpipe.

In the plain and at the ford two armies face each other; are they those of the Magi? Some of the riders are wearing Oriental dress.

Beyond, near the wall, a couple are moving towards the shelter of a hut. The fields are tender green and soft underfoot; in the left panel some peasants are dancing on the grass. But nearer the foreground, behind the donor, amid the ruins of a palace which Brand-Philip considers to be that of Solomon and David, St Joseph is drying the baby's napkins. But the temporary shelter is in a way deceptive: a toad is balancing on the keystone above the door,

only imagined. Balthazar is already kneeling like an officiant, prostrated within the folds of his voluminous red cloak, and is assisted by Melchior, behind whom stands the Moorish king Caspar, followed by a small black maidservant. Some of the gifts have already been given, while others are about to be offered. In these delicate pieces of gold-work, these exquisitely embossed and chiselled articles, we can find the first symbolic meanings.

Balthazar has put down beside his helmet, the mark of his dignity—and on which two birds are shown pecking a berry, meaning lust— a triumph of gold-work showing the sacrifice of Isaac, so heavy that it is crushing the toads of heresy.

Melchior's robe is adorned with a silver collar on which is represented the visit of the Queen

and small devil-figures appear in acrobatic positions at the base of the columns.

On everything in the misty blue sky shines the warm light of the guiding star; on the gilded hills, on the moonlit idol, on the fields, on the waters, on all nature which is scarcely ruffled by the portents, on the city whose strange cylindrical and ovoid buildings seem to have human shapes full of watchful eyes.

It is not anti-nature in the Prado *Epiphany*; but Bosch lets a vague uneasiness filter even in the most sweet and tranquil nature.

The struggle between God and the devil, between truth and trickery, becomes a cruel and bottomless abyss in the pictures with large figures which show the torments of Christ: the London *Christ Crowned with Thorns* (1510, National Gallery) and the Prado painting of the same name, with the figure of Christ motionless between the clashing lines of the hired ruffians, fitted between the faces of the soldiery, which are almost deformed, like leather theatrical masks; or the Ghent *Christ Carrying the Cross* (1515, Museum of Fine Arts) crowded beyond the bounds of probability with hideous, deformed faces. In these aspects of treachery the *horror vacui* does not come from the fantastic or dreamlike visionary quality which is a fertile source of monsters, but from the bitter consciousness that men, in their injustice and perversity, identify themselves with the devil. In the sinister gleam of enamelled and metallic colours, deceit spreads overwhelmingly, and takes shape in the grotesque exaggeration of the profiles, overflowing the pain of the world which, following a diagonal axis from right to left, is reflected in the agony of the Good Thief, in the unfathomable melancholy of Christ, in the troubled memory of Veronica.

We can also date from his last years, around 1510, another significant painting which takes up again a theme already dealt with in the *Triptych of the Haywain*. Whether it is the *Prodigal Son* (Rotterdam, Boymans van Beunigen Museum) in an unusual iconography, or the "wandering fool", the vagabond who does not know who he is nor where to go, or, as "son of Saturn" (Brand-Philip) he stands for the melancholy human and the element earth, the man expresses all the irresolvable sadness of his condition. To return to his father's house, to seek salvation, he leaves behind the herd of pigs of which he was guardian, the house of pleasure with the sign of the swan and the jug fastened to the roof, and takes the road he has chosen— beyond the legendary crossroads, symbol of free will—with odd shoes, bands badly tied, clothes torn (and, as usual, at the knee), a poor cat-skin hung from his knapsack and objects with various meanings, even sexual, as his baggage. Everything expresses a dragging poverty and the painful feelings which have prematurely aged his face. From above, his steps are watched by the heretical owl and the woodpecker, symbol of the Saviour.

But with a point more subtle and mature than in the youthful *Cure for Folly*, the circular shape of the painting seems to draw the observer's glance to the landscape in the background, to the reality of a familiar nature which, in its monochrome stillness, prolongs beyond every episodic meaning, the life of the picture, which begins and anticipates the greatest achievements of Dutch painting.

From Bosch's principal works (the list of which today comprises barely seventy pictures) we can see the artist's stylistic and conceptual progress, always intensely and inevitably interwoven. Throughout his work he broods on the irreparable sadness of the mind, overwhelmed by the forces of evil, paying its debts, both moral and imaginative, in a figurative language of high and unrepeatable originality.

Chapter VIII

THE ARTIST AND HIS PUBLIC

The wide popularity of Bosch's work, presenting and illustrating as it did the intellectual and moral problems of the day, is shown by the frequent copies made of his pictures and by his many imitators and followers; but his work also had an important vehicle in engraving, either in the contemporary transcriptions of Alaert de Hameel, who was a friend of the painter and one of the architects of the Cathedral of 's-Hertogenbosch, or in the later ones from the Paris workshop of Hieronymus Cock, sought after and quickly sold on the European markets.

If these pages make especially obvious Bosch's inventive power, in the variety and the bold novelty of his paintings and the exactitude with which the obscure meanings are presented, they lead us to assume that he appealed to a special public who were interested in the denunciation of the oppression of freedom of conscience, in a reaction to the pressures of the religious authorities, against whom there seems to arise a long-smouldering intolerance because of their theological rigidity and their moral corruption.

In the field of religious themes Bosch may well have been concealing all his complex sources of knowledge, from Jewish gnosis to hermetic symbolism—all this in the elaborate setting of punishments and equally menacing temptations, in a certain way answering the needs of the public, who were accustomed to the familiar though terrible entertainment of processions and tortures, popular festivals and terrifying sermons.

That is why invented pains and horrors are so minutely described and animated; the hell that threatens sinners is not so very remote and different from the events people have seen with their own eyes, or magnified in their imagination to an enormous size; in any case not far from the minds of the public for whom Bosch's paintings and the engravings taken from them were intended.

Among the best known are those of the *Besieged Elephant*, derived, if not from a painting, at least from a drawing by Bosch, engraved by de Hameel with the inscription "bosche" and later (1601) by H. Cock, who noted on it "Hieronimus Bos inve". Crowded with incredible machines of war, the work refers perhaps to Eleazar's battle against an armed and aggressive elephant of the pagan army; we should not forget that an elephant was shown in the Netherlands for the first time in 1484 (Hannema).

Another successful engraving was that of *St Martin*, published by Cock and then by J. Galle, taken from a drawing by Bosch. This bears on the copper plate "J. Galle excud.—H. Bosch inventor" and has an inscription at the top: *La vie joyeuse et sans souci des estropiés* (The joyful and carefree life of the cripples) followed by some lines of verse:

*"Contemple ung peu tous ces boiteaux
Au beau milieu de leur misere
Rire et danser estre joyeux
Sans se soucier de la guerre."*

The key to the whole composition, which took its subject from a mystery play on the life of St Martin, often given in Flanders, is in the Dutch inscription along the base of the sheet, with a French translation underneath: *St Martin pensant faire aux pauvres charité causa par son manteau la guerre aux estropiés* (St Martin, thinking he was being charitable by giving his cloak, caused a fight among the cripples). The scandal of charity.

The cripples follow and besiege St Martin who, in this world of equals, where all are unfortunate, has by giving a cloak to one of them aroused the desire for gain in those who have had nothing: "the gift unasked for is a source of hate and death, it is the cause of the claim to gifts" (Castelli).

Is it better, then, not to show charitable love, and leave them in ignorance of the possibility of good?

Bosch's bitter query leaves open and unresolved the burning questions of his time, torn as it was by the problems of faith and religious struggles. Thus St Martin's figure is barely isolated by the artist's rapid strokes. Around him is every sort of misery. The "cripples" who, before the revelation of his charity were "carefree" and in their own way lived a "joyful life" in ignorance of any other possible happiness, now become truly repulsive in the querulous and obsessive claims which exaggerate their deformities and make them near relatives of the freaks of an imaginary anti-nature.

And the Saint's charity is very near to the sin of pride.

Chapter IX

THE AESTHETICS OF BOSCH

The character and development of Bosch's language is something which happens within the painting itself: a gradual working out of form until it becomes fixed and definite would not only contradict the intrinsic qualities of his art, but would find no corroboration in the analysis of the works. The artist's main interest is to communicate, and thus fulfil the demands of his public, developing to an ever increasing depth the construction of symbols and the forging of links between them, even at the cost of touching on archaic images at first perhaps inexplicable, but in reality strictly relative to the boldness of symbols and forms. It is precisely for that reason that the focus of the painting is not given so much by the lines of convergence in space to which the action can be subordinated, but rather by the central theme, a brilliant centre of attraction around which the meaning of the picture is radially expressed in a fabric of symbols and images all connected with the main theme.

Within these general lines lies the evidence of a wide and articulate knowledge, which involves every aspect of the culture of the time, particularly the esoteric and hermetic, and is in every way extremely sensitive to mysterious gnoses and pre-dogmatic (rather than extra-dogmatic) doctrines. It is sifted by intense meditation in which every aspect of knowledge finds its point of contact in the world of images. This is one of the main justifications for the large number of copies and imitations and, at the same time, the absence of a real circle of pupils, since even his best known successors, such as Mundyn or Huys, do not inhabit the complex world that nourished the vision of the great solitary of 's-Hertogenbosch. It is a heritage that easily exhausts itself in the ever-flowing streams of its fantasy: it reappears only after two generations in the logical and mordant symbolism of Pieter Bruegel the Elder; while the natural atmospheric light of his work lasted long enough to be the undeniable foundation of the Dutch landscapes of the seventeenth century.

To reduce Bosch's composite figurative world to a "factory" of devils is surely to ignore the creative independence of the artist in as much as it reflects, with the deepest consciousness, the social, religious and psychological reality of the world of Holland and of the North in general, at that time of extravagant mediaeval allegories and obscure symbols, sketched in forms that are bizarre and demoniacal, fantastic and visionary, yet always sustained by a spirit of modern irony. If, in fact, the painter still retains a mediaeval conception of the universe which no longer seeks order but constantly breaks up into a chaos that pitilessly lays bare the torment of a man winning or compromising his own salvation, we find in Bosch's work the tragic religious situation of his time, just before the Reformation.

For this reason the beauty of Bosch's images is not in the little figures that sometimes seem to come straight out of illuminated manuscripts; but because everything reaches out towards the beauty of a possible revelation, towards the possession of a freer and more independent knowledge.

Thus the perfection of the figures, in which a mediaeval flavour often persists, is vitalised and renewed by an acute psychological penetration which not only pervades the arrangement of figures in the composition, but extends to take in the view of nature as well.

In this way Bosch's paintings are the evidence of a consciousness of evil suffered, to such an extent that we can suppose personal knowledge and experience: a conceptual and aesthetic world that escapes the net of a circumscribed interpretation and achieves understanding of all the voices that in a sort of apotropaic exorcism seek to defeat the fear of man, alone in the face of the eternal questions of revelation and salvation.

For that reason, then, the symbol tends to overstep its limits and take on the whole of a meaning which, though it may remain partly secret is the identification of a reality which goes beyond the evidence of the senses. And every one of Bosch's works is all the more difficult to understand because the synthesis between the ideological content and the quality of the style, and between the veil of iconography and the hidden background of allusions, can never leave out even one of these elements, or it will miss one of the aspects of its unique artistic originality.

In reality, in this "inventory of the invisible" all the parts acquire an equal importance: everything contributes to the construction of the work, as the introduction of a variant produces a variation of meaning and thus the possibility of a new interpretation. The "civilization of the image" was, in Bosch's time, extraordinarily rich and vital: in it was the image of the world. And in his paintings there is a progress towards a knowledge that actually comes before the image: it is those who know how to look who can make the comparison.

This design for intense meditation is seen not only in certain circular paintings or in *The Seven Deadly Sins*, the shape of which, like that of the Buddhist "mandala" centres the eye and the mind in the intuition of the spiritual law, but it is found also in those triptychs in which the monochrome outer wings create a focus of interest and concentration on cosmic visions which then open on to the brilliant revelation of the painter's vision.

It is a vision and a dream-state: through it man regains part of his history, of his inward life, neither hallowed nor ignored, a field of exploration opening on to a new cosmogony: therein lies the relationship between instruction and initiation, in the gradually rising levels of communication with the observer.

Behind appearances lurk hidden meanings. Man's thirst for knowledge has many chances of penetrating to them, by the power of visual and intellectual persuasion offered by the images. Curiosity for the arcane seeks its own path to knowledge, though aware that some symbols, rooted in a remote and secret learning, cannot easily be deciphered, and only permit the main theme to be caught in the midst of an enigma.

"Marvellous inventor of things fantastic and bizarre" (L. Guicciardini), Bosch was able to resolve his pessimism about man's destiny in the quest for an improbable—an impossible—happiness, in a unique language of contemplative and enchanting poetry.

CONCLUSION

The complexity of Bosch's world prevents us from fully penetrating the many experiences which gave birth to his strange language, highly charged with meaning. But still more problems present themselves to the investigator, such as the basic elements of the formation and peculiar development of his style, and how he rediscovered and adapted his forerunners, and everything that shaped and determined his art. It is a difficult investigation, because of the way he dovetailed and superimposed different conceptual and figurative themes, yet clothing them all in forms that were necessary threads in his fantastic web.

Many scholars have tended to stress the predominance of one strand or another and to seek the key in one direction only. But, to concentrate the attention on one aspect only of Bosch's store of symbolic and allusive images is always to miss something. In fact not one of the artists of the generation nearest to him could restate Bosch's ideological and formal synthesis in terms that were not purely external and narrative; it was only later that it contributed vitally to the supreme irony of Bruegel's human comedy.

Often modern critics, following the propensities of some artists, have tended to move their attention from Bosch's world, seeking to adapt it to their own imaginative explorations rather than to see it as corresponding with the spiritual and cultural climate which was a fertile substratum to Bosch's painting. They have even found affinities with the Surrealists, though it is difficult to give precise expression to the relationships existing in the mental and emotional life of an artist living in a time of anguish and doubt at the turn of the fifteenth and sixteenth centuries. If a hermetic interpretation is possible for the "mysterious" works of Giorgione, and any of the uneasy paintings of the Mannerist school can be seen in the light of alchemy and magic, just as from the end of the last century to the moderns—that is to say, from the Symbolists to Mondrian, from the Futurists to Kandinsky, from the Surrealists to Klee—a hermetic and esoteric trend has been shown to re-emerge, all this only confirms the ferment and power of suggestion of a source ever rich in implications, which, however much iconography may change, is always difficult to express.

There remains, however, the fact that Surrealism has borrowed from Bosch a certain inventive originality; but Bosch's ability to create an original style in the demoniacal sphere of anti-nature, is in the moderns reduced by the difference of circumstances and needs to a sort of distorted adulteration of reality, in a cultural situation which differs in both motivation and results.

They are all different, in fact—the contradictions of the times and the very resources of the spirit. But it is undeniable that Bosch, in his effort to draw out the deep and secret desires rooted in the unconscious, had opened the way, from Bruegel, Rembrandt and Rubens, to all the power of expression of modern man, pledged to redeem his spiritual and intellectual independence. Even to speak of visionary imagination is, once again, to see only part of Bosch: in the nocturnal terror of the *Temptations* as in the fevered visions of demons, in the anguish of nightmare as in the menace of warning, in the complex patchwork of symbolism as in the forked paths of heterodoxy, lay his idea of the world; and, in it, the unique and unrepeatable stamp of his painting.

Child Playing
Kunsthistorisches Museum, Vienna

ALCHEMY

Since it is defined as the science of the arcana, is alchemy therefore one of Bosch's sources? The *Alchemical Man* of the Albertine is one of the key figures.

While Bosch, constrained to keep the secret, evokes a wealth of enigmas in a cryptographic language, one of the "mysteries" impossible to reveal concerns his own life, and especially his complex sexual life. On this subject it is fair to speak of an "androgynous chain", assuming a multiplicity of opposites.

Other alchemical themes are: the hybrids, the egg, the Virgin and the solar disc (*St John on Patmos*), the child Mercury (Lisbon *Temptation of St Anthony*), the crow, the lamb, the stone (*St John the Baptist*), the smiths of hell, Prometheus, the Antichrist; the cosmic landscapes subjected to Vulcan and Mars; Solomon's seal; metals, mineralogy, the jug, the sphere, the *Herbarius*, the key of the simple and Hermes; Halcyon, the child with the windmill and the senile child in the walking frame; the nudes and elements emerging from the hollow tree, one of the themes of the *Temptations*.

The influence on Bosch of the magical and alchemical doctrines of Ruysbroek (1293–1381) who lived in the forest of Soignes in about 1343, is recognised.

Because of the "hermetic secret" it is not easy to fix the relationships between art and alchemy, but there is an obvious relationship between alchemy and the German mystics who sought the secret of life. (1)

The *armed knight* (St George, St Michael) recalls the fight against the *dragon*, but he would appear to have the purpose of determining the sex of the embryo (he faces the monsters). The function of fire and the colour red in Bosch could be explained in this way: it would add an esoteric background to the terrors of the era, which is not surprising; and so it is, even with work in the fields which has had a disturbing aspect from the first use of the harrow. But there is no need to "hide the secrets of agriculture" (also in the *Icarus* of Bruegel?).

Still more disconcerting is the representation of the *alchemical headgear* of the tray resting on the head of the *Tree-man*, and oval in shape, and the "tree of Noah", certainly related to the legend of Abraham. Vessel and "tower" constitute the cosmic furnace (2), the brain "chooses with full autonomy what it needs". (3)

For us today there is an obvious link in this triad: art—alchemy—psychoanalysis. When there are *groups*, as in the Lisbon *Temptation of St Anthony*, a figure appears with his head embedded in a *hollow oak*, dry, bristling with spikes, another image of the alchemist's furnace. As for the alchemical marriage (*Garden of Delights*, Prado), it is also a sexual fantasy and meditation.

Since alchemy is *colour*, it is probable that *The Infernal Concert*, with all its instruments, indicates a series of operations, one of which, the *tree*, is characteristic of melancholy, being the "lunar state".

In *The Alchemical Man*, an exciting figure, rich in meanings, the woman is listening, turning her back, since the purpose of the operation is birth.

Thus we can throw some light on the instruments and their form: the alembic which allows transformation, the matrix, which is to give birth to the *filius philosophicus*, perhaps Isaac. In this cryptographic way we find another link between alchemy and Judaism.

Without attempting to compile an index of the notions implicit in Bosch's alchemical symbolism, we should however observe the following elements, which belong to the secret realms of alchemy, the science of the arcane.

There are the fountain, the unicorn, the egg, the crystal phial, the vase, the crown and the hat; the kingfisher, the baby, the walking-frame, the hollow tree; the crow or *Nigredo* (*St John on Patmos*); the hermit's hut, with the hollow tree corresponding to the athanor, the Grotto, the rock (mineral) and the hollow of *The Alchemical Man* in the Albertine. There are the Virgin and Child (*Epiphany*), the fire; crucible, operations and cucurbit (*Garden of Delights*), the Fountain of Life, coral (*Garden of Delights*) and the Pythagorean ypsilon (central panel), the ladder and the *Mutus Liber* (steps); the pendulum, so enigmatic, which we have studied among the objects.

There is the fawn or the newborn infant, the lamb (enigma of the palm), the M engraved on the knife, and the sulphur, the skull and the Christ Crucified. INRI may mean *Igne Natura Renovatur Integra*, or, in the Rosicrucian sense, the rank of Knight.

Finally there are the key, both in *The Infernal Concert* and *The Conjuror*, the egg, which is also part of the gnosis; the colocynth; the furnace or "experimental cucurbit" (in the Ghent *St Jerome*); the *Pelican*, the name of a vessel, which has been noted by Fraenger, and the ibis, Thoth and Hermes.

The intermingling of the various sysmbolisms does not cause the meanings to be confused, but stabilises their multiplicity.

Thus, for example, the ibis signifies memory, for Castelli (4) the symbol of memory of past pleasures.

The letter M, which is found in *The Garden of Delights*, could be an allusion to the *Liber Mundi* of Christian Rosenkreutz—a secret rebirth in Bosch's time of the tradition which reappears with Luther (his emblem is a heart pierced by a cross, surrounded by a rose) and with Michael Maier (1568–1622).

On the other hand, M symbolises sex, both in astrology (the scorpion) and in alchemy (sulphur). We have noted the part played by the Scorpion, the emblem of the Jews, and in a way that of Bosch, who was born under that sign.

Finally, without supporting the thesis that he was a forerunner of the Scottish school, as Dürer appears to have been (at least in his self-portrait, *The Knight with the Thistle*) we have to recognise that in Bosch it is very strange to find *The Knight with the Thistle* (*distel*) as against the goldfinch (in Dutch, *distelvink*), which it phonetically resembles.

Thus meanings interweave and entangle, forming a gnosis constructed in a thousand ways, all such as to represent faith in reason. The essential is to admit and understand the spirit of an era, the reality of the psyche of a man of that time.

Still in the field of alchemy, as regards the representation of crenellated shapes and enclosures, we can admit the validity of these fortified, battlemented structures to indicate the phenomena of inversion and isolation. (5)

ANTICLERICAL

According to Lucien Febvre it would be a contradiction in terms to speak of irreligion, but how are we to explain the spirited anticlerical movement that was widespread in Northern Europe at this time?

Undoubtedly we find in Bosch "a harsh satire on the Church" (6). It is typical of the period; the "budding of the Reformation" was already felt in the anticlerical movements, beginning with the denunciation of the corruption of the clergy: nun, monk, *Haywain*, *Conjuror*, *Ship of Fools*. On the opposite side is sanctity: the anchorites, *St Christopher*.

There exist in Bosch's work, "distinct and opposed": "clerical themes" and "anticlerical themes" (7). We cannot forget his polemics against the monks, against those who wear the cowl; it is common knowledge. (The repressive power of the Church is strongly denounced in his pictures of hell.)

Notwithstanding the violent attacks (bottom right hand corner of *The Infernal Concert*) against simony too, this dualism makes Bosch's art the testimony of a period of transition; the acid criticism of the monks and Church dignitaries (in *The Haywain* and by *The Hill-man*) derives from a sense of aggression, from the theme of the Swan, emblem of the sect of the Free Spirit and the anti-monastic attitude (shared later by Erasmus and Luther). At any rate Bosch, who fulminates against the preachers, knows that "religious literature" is the most untruthful.

A lover of truth, Bosch joins the chorus of the faithful of that period, who rose up against the "abuses" (8): simony, the sale of indulgences.

He is anticlerical, but this aspect of his work does not mean atheism.

THE APOCALYPSE

One of Bosch's sources is the Apocalypse, written by St John on Patmos and made up of seven visions, relating to the Millennium, Enoch, Metatron, the Archangel of the Torch, the Revelation. According to René Alleau, the apocalyptic literature of the second and third centuries A.D. "contained the essential elements of the esoteric Jewish–Christian tradition".

Apocalyptic dreams are part of Bosch's tormented and cryptic world, which sometimes seems obsessed by the prophetic vision of the end of the world, or by the Millennium which, after the fall of Antichrist, is to precede the Last Judgment. It is on the Apocalypse that the visionary proposes to base his eschatology.

ARS MORIENDI

The *Ars Moriendi* is one of Bosch's sources, which is not enough to explain the anguish and anxiety, a "new direction impressed on religious thought" (9).

Much has been said about a taste for the macabre in the birth and flowering of the Baroque. In Bosch's time, *L'Art de bien mourir* by A. Vérard (1492) was a very popular work. The Last Days are recorded in *The Seven Deadly Sins* under these themes: Death, Judgment, Hell and Paradise.

In *The Death of the Miser* the door is half open, because souls can enter freely. Avarice demands hell.

BACCHUS

Bacchus or Dionysus is a forgotten or neglected source, like the function of the "four greats" of imaginative art: Hermes, Pythagoras, Orpheus and Saturn.

The enigma of the bees, "wild beings" forced to be incessantly on the move, is explained not through Deborah (10) or the predilection of the swarm for the forest, but the *tree-trunk*. It is known that the tree-trunk "around which the vine twists" is the typical attribute of Bacchus.

Among the symbols of the "god of wine" are—and their very diversity gives them a certain humour—the fig (the leaves of which covered Adam's sex), the laurel, the vine (the place of the vine is the plain; the mountain begins where the vines disappear, and the discovery of the Promised Land in the Lisbon *Temptation* is symbolised by an enormous bunch of grapes carried between two men), the dolphin, the dragon, the panther (yoked to the chariot of Bacchus when he returns from the conquest of India), the phoenix, the cup, the horn, the wreath of vine-leaves (vines have considerable importance in the *Herbarius* of *The Temptations*) and masks.

BANQUETS

In a brotherhood or association, the annual banquet is sumptuous. The feast goes back to its origins, under the symbol of the swan in *The Marriage at Cana* (Boymans) and lets us discover one of the most significant points, the gnostic altar-sideboard, on a base formed of twelve squares, of which four are at the bottom, while the magus is pointing with his wand to the thirteenth, or the second, at the top.

The Marriage at Cana is probably the feast of the initiating brotherhood. Perhaps from that point Bosch takes up the torch of rebellion, preferring to express himself cryptographically, so many pictures of his revealing the doctrines, with a multiplicity of meanings.

The ritual banquets (which perhaps followed the sacrifice of the swan and other animals) had an important function: they corresponded to the "communion sacrifice" which is the most characteristic act of the cult. On the other hand these meals are not innocent. The study of the mysteries, in the true sense of the word, is also that of the *agapae*, which link guests and brethren in a common heritage of knowledge. Symbols and emblems of the altar offer various indications, like the gestures and the presence of the child with the long robe, who wears a sash and is holding up the cup.

One of the few definite scraps of information about Bosch's life concerns the Banquet of the Swan which took place at 's-Hertogenbosch in 1488, when the artist was already an important "master". The ritual *agapae* were established, thanks to the dignity conferred upon Bosch by virtue of his title of official painter to the Brotherhood and perhaps each was served according to the order of a hierarchy.

Banquets and feasts, gargantuan meals, are a sign of power, an expression of joy, of the need to know each other, to taste real savours, to share the pleasure of aromas, to take part in the "alchemy" of the kitchen, which associates the swan with the wild boar. Taking into account the aphrodisiac effect (the swan's flesh has a curious reputation) of rare foods and drink, the banquet, even if it took place in a brotherhood, was not innocent.

In *The Marriage at Cana*, which is perhaps a banquet to celebrate the foundation of a sect (twelve persons are seated at an L-shaped table, and the thirteenth, the child, is standing, and making a salutation or a prayer to those present) a link is formed between the participants by the fact of having something in common. The enigma concerns the gnosis, and perhaps the Johannine love-feast. St John was the patron saint of 's-Hertogenbosch, and the Precursor had instituted baptism: from the Apocalypse to the designation of the Messiah there is such a range of possibilities that imagination naturally steps in.

THE BESTIARY

The bestiary is an inexhaustible subject which makes use of every symbol and shows an exoticism of which we are not always aware. Delight in the fabulous throws off all restraint, and there appears the *hybrid*, the typical creature of a fantastic world. Bosch went a long way along this road, which could be placed under the sign of the basilisk, guardian of the threshold, tamed by adepts and virgins.

In the bestiary of the imagination unheard-of "aberrations" and fables, and scientific intuition and divination, walk side by side to the very limits of *hybris*, stimulating animal and human dynamism and, by dreaming, giving birth to monsters and causing metamorphoses, conquering the universe of terror with the appearance of these strange inventions, which are the work of man.

Bosch, an enthusiastic painter of animals, lost no opportunity of inventing curious beasts. In *The Garden of Delights*, among fierce wild animals, it is impossible to recognise any impressive species of a type unusual then, which we could call "oceanic" or "southern". The "flying dragon", the enormous marsupial, and some prophetic animals including the great ram (in Iran the symbol of glory) are enigmatic.

We do not know the meaning of the prevalence of slimy and hairy beings and beasts armed with spurs, beaks, trunks, unless it means close observation of nature and of exotic species, which leads to the herbivorous insect, with its hard wing-cases, being changed into an aggressive monster.

The beast appears . . . "and it twined around the Prince" (11). But there is another dominant motif: a relationship with the Apocalypse or the demon in the form of a locust; and we should not forget the role of the horse (its skull appears in the cave of the *Temptations*).

We cannot forget certain inexplicable predilections: angel-birds, covered with feathers and hair, yet naked; and it is strange that, without being part of the cycle of the "wild man" of which we shall see the importance, the hairiness proper to the demon is the image of sin.

As examples of aggressiveness there are the bear and the wolf which attack travellers and carry on the fights between animals in the *Earthly Paradise* and the *Triptych of Delights*: the wild boar chases a strange antediluvian beast, which gives us as background a universe of violence, of which we become only gradually aware.

As a work of instruction, the bestiary offers various meanings for the same beast: the kingfisher (*Haywain, Hell*) recalls the dog for etymological reasons and alchemy as a symbol of salt, and it has a generally admitted ethical meaning: it is the sign of vanity. There is a proverb: "when the kingfisher builds its nest, the sea seems calm". It is a bird of good omen: the tower will be

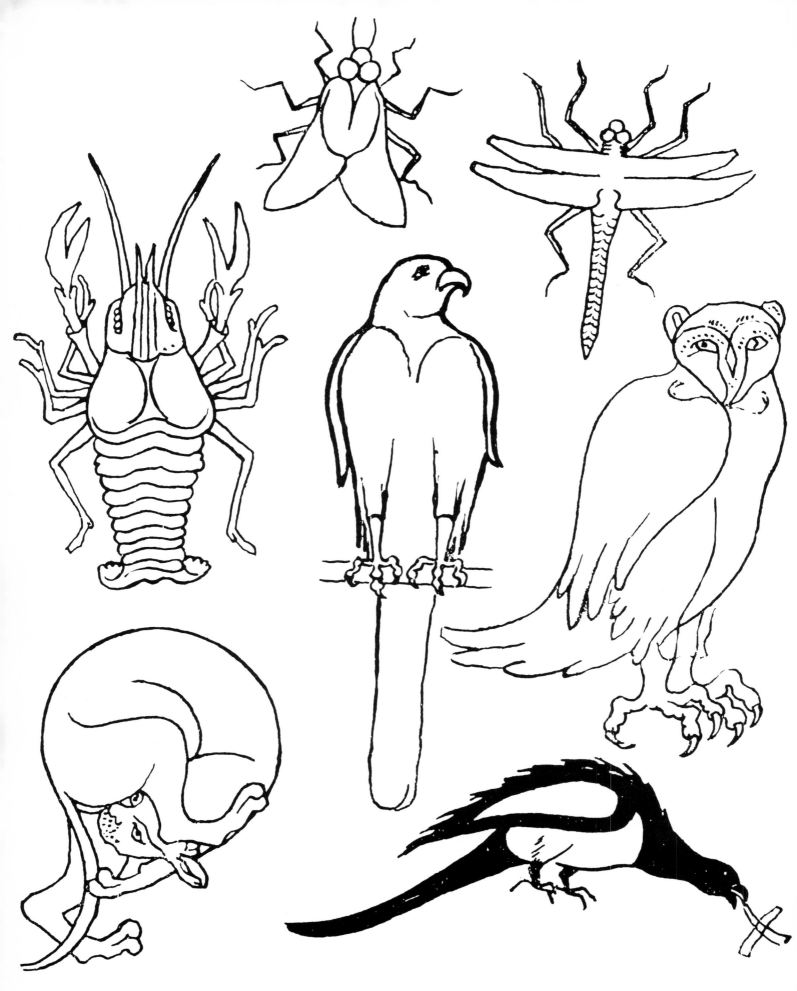

successfully built and in any case work is proceeding apace.

The frog, gnostic like the toad, means lust (*Haywain*), Diopetes, the fall of Jove from Heaven.

The animal stamped on the shield (*Ecce Homo, Christ Carrying the Cross*) is not an emblem of lust, but the mark of the "legion of Satan", the toad. It appears on the knight's standard in *The Garden of Delights* and *Hell*. What does it represent? The symbol of evil, the seed of hell, the alchemical vessel, the guardian of the treasure on the shoulders of the man carrying the tax register on his head in *The Infernal Concert*. The devil was in the habit of appearing in the form of the toad, and he is showing himself thus on the breast of the girl beside the witch.

A curious scene in *The Infernal Concert* has attracted Fraenger's attention (12); it is a toad, spotted, transfixed by a twig—perhaps of hazel—which is burning, so that the "beast", so diabolically tortured, may emit a nauseous stench in the direction of the lute.

At the window of the law court (*Ecce Homo*), in a niche, in the forest, on a tree or on the disc of a fountain, the owl of the philosophers is a landmark which distracts attention from the main scene going on in the path of *The Prodigal Son* or *The Haywain*.

The owl symbolises the science of the occult, the "penetration of the invisible", the quest for wisdom. The association between wisdom and reason is perhaps too binding. The aim would be to "find oneself right to the depths" (13). The owl on the fountain (*Garden of Delights*) means that self-contemplation and self-knowledge derive from one single process: precise concentration.

More generally, the owl is a symbol of wisdom and suggests an ancient gnosis. In *The Alchemical Man* (Albertine) the owl is perched above, at the same level as the green monkey on the ladder, as an inevitable attribute of the tree of life.

This *Tree-man* is the "tree of life" and at the same time of knowledge.

Given these different symbols, Bosch's work could be a manifestation of serious irreverence against dogma or the will of God, making use of a whole network of heresies.

In *The Garden of Delights*, which offers an inexhaustible wealth of symbols, we find the ibis, the salamander (alchemy); birds, emblems of lust and shame according to Tolnay (14); the fishes of the sea, which represent will and anguish, while the oyster is the female symbol. Storks, crows and peacocks are the emblem of sexual pleasure and vanity when they are perched on the bathers' heads or emerging from the anus.

Unusual animals and marvellous plants symbolise all creation before dogma was imposed. But there are two opposing theses according to Panofsky; wild animals represent the "prey of Eros", and the dividing line between beast and man is constantly modified and breached by the "hybrid" which uses natural weapons: beaks, claws, wings.

As for *The Creation of the World* (*Triptych of Delights*), it includes the animals, created from nothing in seven days, among which are the otter, the wild cat, the rabbit, the magpie, the swan, the duck, herds of unicorns, cattle and horses and swirling flights of birds and spirits.

Origene reports some formulas with which to address the spirits "so that the divine element within man might be exalted to divinity by their intercession" (15). Each one stood in relation to a planet and had the head or mask of a beast: lion—Michael; bull—Uriel; serpent—Raphael; eagle—Gabriel; bear—Tatabaoth; dog—Erataoth; ass—Tartaraoth (sacred to Priapus).

In the bestiary we recognise the mixture of innumerable elements taken from various disciplines and themes: alchemy, astology, the zodiac, the gnosis, the Apocalypse, masks, legendary traditions and the influx of a forgotten concept: the admonitory *exemplum*.

The hybrid as a model to imitate—and so much imitated—is a protest against the moralising bestiary. Being supposed to represent vice, it could be allowed every liberty against anything which might restrain it.

Shapes given life and freedom: all figures contrary to virtue swarm threateningly around anyone who aspires to solitude; asceticism seems powerless to conquer the dynamism of hostile forces. And the conflict spreads from the tempted ascetic to the hybrid elements of the *Temptations*; from the vague smile, analogous to that of the judge, to the hidden menaces, while a cataclysm or an irruption threatens. It is the hydra that proliferates, not the hybrid. The hydra is formed from the march of armed and mobile objects which arouse terror—from the assault of all the elements. Perhaps at the beginning of this movement there is a long silent contemplation; everything crowds in on one who waits and observes: the visionary.

Another origin of the bestiary is without doubt dreams and contact with animals. During childhood, the experience of cruelty comes with animals. The closeness of the instinctive and animal (physiological) and the psychical side of our impulses explains the frequency of allegories inspired by animals.

The bull, the horse, the dog, the serpent, give us an idea of nature, of the strength of these impulses. "It is thus easy to interpret the condition of our forces and our sexual appetites" (16).

In mythology, which we tend to forget, the animal appearance "is always a manifestation only, beneath which the personage proper shows through, seen by the eye of the narrator; that is one of the characteristics of archaism" (17).

MUTUS LIBER, IN QUO TAMEN tota Philosophia hermetica, figuris hieroglyphicis depingitur, ter optimo maximo Deo misericordi consecratus, solisque filiis artis dedicatus, authore cuius nomen est Altus.

21. ii. 82. Neg:
93. 82. 72. Neg:
82. 81. 33. Tued.

BROTHERHOODS

Associations and brotherhoods, including meetings with pilgrims, travellers and "philosophers" have a very important function in Bosch's life, despite the scarcity of information at our disposal.

The Brotherhood of Our Lady, called the Company of the Swan, was founded at 's-Hertogenbosch in 1318, and Bosch was admitted into it in 1486. The Brothers of the Common Life or the Order of St John of Jerusalem (perhaps forerunners of the Rosicrucians?) the movement founded by Geert Grote or Groote, settled in 's-Hertogenbosch in 1424. Next came the Brothers of the Free Spirit, Adamites, according to Fraenger, a sect closely studied by Norman Cohn, to which Bosch is supposed to have belonged.

We cannot doubt the spirit of renewal preached by the brotherhoods in the Netherlands "until the end of the fourteenth century" (22).

Groote abandoned "the study of magic" to point the *"way to the forest"*, and that "wilderness", source and seat of temptations, is still wild. On the other hand, the brotherhood which "specialised in the representation of the Mysteries" (23) stimulated the "taste for hell" in a theatrical sense, allowing any licence in this respect. The brotherhoods helped to secularise and popularise sacred themes and those which were performed in the public squares expressed the complexity of the life of the times.

Erasmus, a student at 's-Hertogenbosch for three years, received instruction from the Brothers of the Common Life, who are said to have had links with certain *ante litteram* members of the "Brotherhood of the Rosicrucians" (24). According to P. Arnold, Geert Groote had contact with Christian Rosenkreutz, but the dates and facts are still disputed.

As for the allusions to sects or "secret societies" in *The Marriage at Cana*, according to Bax (25) some details like the swan, the boar, the magus or wizard (sometimes called "priest of Satan") refer to "a Jewish sect which practised a secret cult, learned from the Egyptians or the Syrians".

According to Baltrusaitis, Our Lady is Isis, and the brotherhood of which Bosch was a member carried on numerous activities under the emblem of the swan; among others, it formed the Cathedral orchestra, spread the passion for music, provided ornaments, altarpieces and pictures. According to Delevoy, the brotherhood set up a company "specialising in the organisation of dramatic recitals, the representation of the Mysteries, dances from hell, spectral ballets, farces and stories of devils".

There was thus an "incredible wealth" of accessories, artifices, objects which reappear in the *Temptations* and in the scenes in hell: iron helmets, leather noses, masks of cloth and of calf-hide and sheepskin, embroidered mantles, standards of gold and silk, tallow candles and oil-lamps.

When the brotherhood took part in the procession in honour of Mary (which takes place still on August 15th) one of the carts represented the "Temptation of the Hermit".

Ideologies, beliefs, rites were thus shown through objects; through the brotherhoods it was possible to know the secret life. Though undoubtedly very busy, Bosch took part in certain acitivities which are mysterious to us. As a member of a brotherhood, his works of art would have had an informative function within the community. With an intellectual basis that is largely lost to us, they were appreciated by an audience who were "in the know".

Some ancient brotherhoods had magic and military initiations, which may have conjured up demons, brigands, heroes and werewolves in the imagination, which embody man at his most savage. And this throws on demonology, which is obviously not excluded from Bosch's work, a more complex and different light from the obsessions of the clergy and the Inquisition, or even of the people.

BUBBLES

The elements—water, air, fire and winds—are, as it were, the natural cornerstones of the world of imagination, which lives on excesses. The man of the sixteenth century was still close to nature and may have imagined the strangest things.

The gigantic bubble, limiting the space around it, is typical of the world of fantasy in Bosch. It is often a home for a couple "imprisoned" inside it. The protecting crystalline wall is isolating, and whatever does not penetrate into it becomes part of another world.

A translucent bubble encloses the hybrids; it is a bubble which circumscribes their visual field, in which everything visible is enclosed: the hybrids' bubble is their universe.

When we think of this image today we realise its timeless symbolism, for we all exist in "bubbles enclosing each of us in our own world" (26). We and our neighbours are all surrounded by invisible bubbles.

BUFFOONS

Among Bosch's characters and sources, buffoons have an important place. The "wise fool" is a madman, and the "foolish mother" a satire on the Church.

The brotherhood's buffoon was present among the actors of a Mystery or other theatrical performances. The squatting buffoon is an exhibitionist, and the behind, called the "negative front" are shown off in order to insult the adversary—an indication of the frequent rivalry between neighbouring communities. At Goslar there is a column surmounted by a figure in this pose (27).

This exhibition of the backside, pretending to be a face, is the reason why the devil wears a mask in that part of the body. There are connections, both theatrical and feudal, between the licentious buffoon and the devil.

THE COSMOS

In Bosch everything concerning the universe is represented in various ways: heaven, earth and sea (*Garden of Delights*); subterranean world; paradise, millennium, hell.

There is an aspect which commentators often forget: the chthonic (from the Greek *khthon*: earth). The earth (*Garden of Delights*) is identified with hell and seems to be considered as the origin of monsters. But the hybrids are not peculiar to the earth; in the *Temptations* the air is peopled with monsters moving at will. The universe is inhabited on various planes.

Bosch uses a long-abandoned cosmological system: the orbis, belonging to an ancient philosophy of nature, that floats "like a disc inside a sphere". The cosmic symbols include: the circle ("scene of the Passion" on the back of *St John on Patmos*); the globe (in grisaille) and the theme of the world reflected "in the iris of the divine eye".

As for the concept of the universe divided into various planes, we have to note the "diagrammatic" composition and the progression of the *Seven Deadly Sins*, which represent the history of man being led to hell by his passions.

The universe is not without its magic aspect. In his own way Bosch applies the formula of Pythagoras: "All is number", beginning with the use of the grid, as in the Albertine *Alchemical Man*.

But not everything is simply magic and technique. Bosch studies the phenomena of transparency (*Garden of Delights*), and symbolises the purity of life and love in crystal tubes and glass globes, in the ampoules of the Fountain of Life: this fountain reveals the exuberance of nature. In Bosch, the cosmos, the world are indissociable.

CRIPPLES

We can never insist enough on the function in Bosch's art of crowd scenes, the race of beggars and cripples, not to mention the "beghards", heretics who lived on alms. The Church festivals, and the alley-ways or the main square, were the kingdom of the beggars. In Bosch's time, the expression "*cour des miracles*" or "brotherhood of beggars" is significant; physical suffering accustomed people to "terror and anguish" (28). The "cagneux" (cripples, from the Latin *canis*, dog, and man without shame) suffered starvation, and their only preoccupation was to satisfy their hunger.

Bosch understood the world of cripples. In the *Temptations of St Anthony* there is an intriguing figure: the magus, recognisable by his tall hat and wand, is guarding or pointing at a severed foot lying on a cloth in front of him. Perhaps we should see in this scene a reversal of functions: the people have sometimes seen "in certain saints those responsible for some disease" (29). Robert Gaguin describes beggars thus: "St Pius makes them lame and paralytic".

In this respect, Bosch's work is rooted in the Middle Ages; beggars lived in caves and hovels, emerging to demand alms from pilgrims and mingling wherever crowds gathered.

CRUELTY

One of the characteristics of cryptographic art is the use of a "moralistic scene", such as hell. It is also an illustration of the customs of the time which might shock us now, but which were then judged normal.

Bosch denounces unrelentingly the cruelty of the demons (Lisbon *Temptation*). His work is a history of cruelty and torture, inspired by the Inquisition. Pain, torture, the activity of the devourer (*Garden of Delights*), sensuality and cruelty dominate the whole. It is devoted to the enumeration of sins, but it is also a study of the instruments of repression and the sadistic pleasures of the clergy, of the executioner, the "devil" and demons. To this bill of indictment is added the cruelty of the crowd (*Ecce Homo*). We cannot call this spiteful, armed, envious assembly "the Jews", or at least not if we are to understand the attitude of Bosch, who could denounce the anti-semitism that was already rife.

Cruelty and theatricals go hand in hand, but not without strange bursts of violence. Seizing the opportunity of the performance of a Mystery play, archers surrounded the ghetto; the actors' skill was so persuasive that there was a dangerous outbreak. People enjoyed executions in the public squares or on the neighbouring hill of execution which often dominated a city and was a sign of power. According to Huizinga, "the end of the Middle Ages became a period of judicial cruelty" (30).

In the last few centuries Bosch's work has been judged without thinking, or caring to think about that period; even though we study the *diableries*, born, it is believed "simply in the artist's imagination".

His own time was no longer content with the help of pious minds and "good thoughts". We are in a position to judge and to understand, provided that we do not cover our faces before a disturbing message: the aggression and repression we have before our eyes. Bosch had seen this aggression and repression "in the acts of his contemporaries", and the anguish he portrays,

his pessimism about human nature, are based on fact.

There is one character which, in a curious way, represents cruelty as attacked by Bosch: the judge.

Uneasy, tormented in a situation of conflict, but authoritative, despite his expression (the meaning of which cannot always be understood, except for his hypocrisy: "You see, I cannot do otherwise"), the judge embodies the sadism that is legal in society; he is the accomplice of executioners and demons.

The distance separating the characters—the judge from the martyr—makes it possible to show a cruelty which is all in the glance and reveals the turbulent background of hagiography. Bosch knew how to use it in his works. He is really more interested in the hybrids in his pictures than in the lives of the saints, because the hybrid's grotesqueness is so much more expressive.

In contrast with moralistic views there are horrible visions: the perfection of a world of devourers and impalers. Everything in the field of torture is regulated: every fault, every sin has its corresponding punishment, imposed by the judge or the Inquisition.

These revenges wreaked on the body are really dreadful; this discrediting of everything concerning the body; this intolerable series of judicial systems in the service of the Church and of repression, in the "witch-hunt" and the persecution of heretics, under cover of respect for the superiority of dogma (any scene from the *Deadly Sins* is an anthology of tortures either legal or tolerated by dogma); this way of provoking fear by concentrating on a horror which could be salutary. What sort of a religion of love is this, which has been able to tolerate terror to such a point? Is this intended to convince, or is it a way to express the cruelty of both clergy and feudal lords?

Did this truth in Bosch's work, his denouncing of the judicial system which had become a show in public squares, show through his other moral themes? His images of cruelty and horror have a strange obsessive power.

DECANS

With regard to hermetic science and astrology (the Tarot, certain sword-blades, and other sources of Bosch's art are partly derived from these "techniques"), hermetic teaching on the Decans is generally passed over in silence, perhaps through ignorance, as is the function of the *Herbarius*, the doctrine of the thirty-six plants corresponding to the thirty-six decans, which can be observed at the base of certain pictures.

In a structure, and particularly that of the sphere (W. Deonna has studied some symbolic meanings of the circle, the sphere, the wheel "in relationship to the living being") (31) and the globe, the decans are "the rulers over ten" (degrees of the circle and ellipse). There are three decans for every sign of the Zodiac (Decanus is the genius, undoubtedly a demon, which governs every ten) and there are thirty-six for the whole circle (360°). Their dominion extends to space and time. Every decan rules over ten days: they watch over the twelve night hours.

Hermetic tradition on the Decans is as ancient as the first works on astrology, going back to Hermes. There is a certain hieratic quality, unobserved up to now, in the relationship between decans and characters (three for each sign of the Zodiac) with feet from which the head emerges, holding up "the outer circle of the world" (and which can be seen in the upper part of some works like the Vienna *Triptych of the Last Judgment*, and in the central panel and inner part of the left panel of *The Haywain*) while they touch the circle of the Zodiac with their feet.

According to hermetic teaching, the influence of the decans works upon us (and from this derives popular astrology, though supplemented from other sources); the decans give out forces called "daughters of the decans" and similar to "demons", or shoots called *tanes*, or they generate stars called "hypoliturgic".

There is, therefore, a whole series of images concerning the bodily appearance of the personified decans, of which the *tanes* are the rays. These images have passed into Egyptian art, a remote, but active and surprising source (Egyptian costume partly explains the *Temptations*). The rays of the sun are compared to hands stretching out to the earth to gather the perfume of the plants. The *tanes* then acquire another meaning: they are the fluids emitted by these rays, and the energies emanating from the work and picked up by the artist are not chimeras.

One of the aims of this knowledge is to ensure "salvation", and it actually seems that Bosch's work admits of other forms of salvation besides the Christian one. His mysterious images and strange figures could represent the knowledge and beliefs of the adepts of the Free Spirit.

DEMONOLOGY

Demonology, though one of the sources of the scenes in hell or the *Temptations*, does not, however, reflect all their content, which is infinitely complex, even to becoming a doctrine.

In the usual meaning, accepted by J. Tondrieu and R. Villeneuve, demonology is "the scientific study of demons, supplementing theology or theodicy, the study of God". Among Bosch's favourite characters are Satan and the devils, who have "knowledge of all things" and derive from it their power on earth (scenes of temptation) and in hell (scenes of torture). They justify the presence on earth of the Magi, who are here "to witness to the existence of demons and angels".

There is a whole demonic hierarchy, known also to Bruegel, and a classification according to "species" or wings (of strange butterflies, armies or "hordes" on the march, another component of this terrifying bunch).

The "figures" each have a name which relates to the deadly sins: Lucifer represents pride; Mammon avarice; Asmodeus lust; Satan anger; Beelzebub gluttony, and he is certainly a "devourer" but in this vice he is often replaced by Behemoth; Leviathan envy; Belphagor vanity and sloth.

The whole topology of fantastic art is revealing: the demons, creatures of the "wilderness", frequent forests, caverns, (the cave becomes the entrance into the subterranean, hidden world), underground passages and fields.

For want of a "wilderness", of which few were known at that time, witches and demons meet in forest glades for their "orgies" and Sabbats.

In reality the influence of the Mystery plays on Bosch's work is remarkable. The making of designs, and perhaps carvings, the choice of costumes and masks together with accessories, has had a lasting effect. We cannot forget, on the other hand, the importance of stories told in the night or by the fire, full of strange suggestions and "visions" which may depend on the witches' ointment or some hallucinogen.

DIONYSUS

Dionysus and the "Grecian realm" imagined by the pre-humanist spirit, is among the inspirations of the Brotherhood of the Free Spirit.

Probably Dionysus was first of all the personification of a *sacred king*, at least that is the thesis of Robert Graves (32) "whom the goddess ritually killed with a thunderbolt in the seventh month from the winter solstice, and whom her priestesses devoured". In Bosch, the myth of the "devourer" may allude to the old rite of eating human flesh, which recurs in his work in the scenes in hell.

It is probable that in the *Triumph of Dionysus* there is a suggestion of the fact that wine replaces other stimulants, but our knowledge of these matters is too limited.

Banquets and wedding feats suggest the idea of a "conversion" since the Dionysiac learning and the revival of Jewish studies are part of a strange mysticism.

According to the doctrine of the *Three Ages of Humanity* by Jacobello del Fiore, famous for its Dionysiac trend, the reign of the Son (perhaps celebrated in the *Garden of Delights*) is expressed in spring, wine, the ear of wheat and the dawn.

DIVINATION

Divination, or the art of predicting the future and causing unusual phenomena, is carried out by means of instruments, objects, ingredients dice and ciphers, numerology, the science of ciphers, which are little known to the layman.

To define the importance of divination in Bosch's art would be an undertaking rich in surprises. We know the function of the magician, the gipsy, the "cabalist", the philosopher or sage, the alchemist.

Magicians and fortune tellers provide "medicines", herbs, hence the unsuspected importance of the *Herbarius*, even in the figures and landscapes of the Rotterdam *St Christopher*.

In its different aspects, divination constitutes an unexpected form of paganism, and of the penetration of the Orient at the decline of the Middle Ages.

Magicians, wizards, wise men, alchemists, Jews, fortune-tellers, jugglers multiply or increase the temptations (we could collect from works of art up to Bruegel an astounding catalogue of heresies and sects, still largely unresearched); temptations which assail the saint and hermit or the ribald and licentious cleric. Bosch's thought expresses itself in the slightest details,

in the complicated fabric of symbols.

The gnosis known to Bosch and practised by him, and put into his work, in the pre-Reformation spirit, was aimed at causing clerical "learning" to fall into disuse. Gnostic thought, already formed and exceptionally rich, was growing by the convergence of various doctrines.

And note the multiplicity of systems of divination implying a specific technique, geomancy (known to the magus of the *Temptations*) and a "universal" practice: astrology, often forgotten when listing sources.

Bosch gives us a picture, more or less veiled beneath the apparent indictment, of the practitioners of divination in his time: the magician, the gipsies, the juggler, the charlatan, defining the position of the "individual" in society, together with the crowd and the fairs.

This quest for the unusual, even in jest, leads to the establishment of relationships between the symbol and the cosmos. Perhaps at its origins—at least among the Arabs—divination was a sacred science. The practice of divination is part of a complex of technical and ritual knowledge, and includes the study of monstrosities, which explains the taste of the period for strange animals and plants. On the other hand—and it is certainly a great paradox—Cicero, who was very much in fashion in the sixteenth century, offered his readers, in the *De Divinatione*, some very effective lessons in rationalism.

DONORS

The donor signifies the presence of the layman in a religious scene. In the Prado *Epiphany*, the kneeling person on the left is Peter Bronckhorst, whose coat of arms, identified by Lafond in 1914, is surmounted by the motto: ENN VOER AL (Each for all).

The scene of the shepherds carrying the lamb, or the implicit sponsorship of St Agnes or St Anthony permit an alternation of the layman and the patron saint. Thanks to the commissions of the brotherhoods and corporations, a certain secularisation came into Bosch's painting.

THE DRAGON

The dragon or often the serpent is a monster which at one time threatened the "knight" (St George or St Michael) who was lost, or perhaps undergoing an initiation test.

The relationship between the monster and the labyrinth is well known, but there is also the Beast of the Apocalypse. Bosch excels in varying its appearance; his favourite dragon is the devouring kind, or the Old Serpent, the incarnation of Satan.

St George, accepting the ritual initiatory combat, becomes the protector of men, endowed with a power of ubiquity. A special relationship is recognised between St George and the savage world, between the champion and the hybrid in its environment, both endowed with a particular power.

It is not known for what reason, in Bosch's hell, there appear knights who deserve the punishment of impalement; the artist is no lover of feudalism, just as he is far from "clerical". But knighthood has a part in his work, with battles and combats, not to mention cavalcades. But is it in virtue of the fight against the dragon or as an initiation ritual? This is a thesis we can apply to the relationship of the Order of Templars with the Grail and the phoenix, which is part of alchemical symbolism; the red colour of the stone, the liberated mind.

Bosch's commentators too often forget the spiritual sense which emanates from the traditional use of symbols, in contrast with Christian symbolism which seems to have the purpose of destroying the proofs of everything which came before it, proofs which the artist collects with a determination worthy of an adept of the Free Spirit.

As for the dragon and the fight against it, we should not forget the connection with the cup or vessel in the *Temptations* or *The Marriage at Cana*. It is here that the study of symbols reveals the teaching: the victory over the dragon and the inevitable tribulations going before it, ensure the "conquest of immortality" (33) represented by some object which the dragon guards.

As for the mediaeval universe, the world of terrors then evoked, the dualism of anguish and desire is complemented by a *quest* the extent of which we must not forget, celebrated in ancient mythology, the quest for immortality, bound up with the struggle, with the "vessel", with the possession of a drink or a "means of seeing".

This conquest, or the element concerned—possessed and tamed, conquered or used—implies re-integration in the central point of the human personality, or, according to René Guénon, "at the point at which communication is established with the higher states of the being".

One of the sources, reasons and causes of Bosch's "visions" lies in this spirituality, undoubtedly heterodox but real, which implies a cosmology the images of which appear in the *Temptations*, if we can understand their meaning.

DUALISM

According to Fraenger (34) Bosch served two different masters: the Church and a "revolutionary opposition", which also commissioned his works and fought against the dissoluteness of the Church. The disposition of the different elements contradicts itself in the "contrasts" of the work as a whole; but this is no new contest, and Bosch shows exceptional freedom in his gnostic works (elaborating a gnosis) and in the temptation scenes.

As regards the image of Paradise or Eden, notwithstanding the sorcery and enticements of the *Garden of Delights*, the image prevailing is that of Hell, which is in reality a history of punishments required by the Church. (Unconsciously, hagiography reveals many details on the terrors of repression).

In the *Death of the Miser* dualism can be observed between the crucifix and the bag of money; it is seen in the creation of Eve (*Garden of Delights*), between the man who is still "pure" (later he will be impure under the fig-leaf) and the woman "who carries in her body the seed of evil". In Bosch's work, the Church is continually criticised or opposed by his obvious militant Manicheism. God and Satan, light and darkness (but who thought of the cross as a symbol of light before this symbolism, known to Bosch, was rediscovered?) dominate the collection of antithetic views, the last great visionary and encyclopaedic work before the invention of the book. Cryptographically, Bosch shows the conflicts of the human psyche at grips with dogmatic authority.

Bosch's work is an impressive testimony to that meeting of trends and to the crystallisation of conflicts. Dignitaries—pope, emperor, king—follow *The Haywain*, forming its strange rearguard, while the procession moves towards hell.

We must realise that there are no amplified anticlerical statements in the work of Bosch, who was loyal to his period and his brotherhood, to the doctrine of the sects and a tradition which is still to be rediscovered; but life with its truth creates a dilemma. In *The Prodigal Son*, what are we to make of a journey that is undoubtedly a return: hesitation or uncertainty between two roads? A single path is traced, the decision has been taken, before the bridge, after a moment of waiting, with his eyes turned towards an invisible spectator. What is he leaving behind? At any rate it is certainly not the Inn.

EVENTS

Different events are marvellously brought out by Bosch: the *Adoration*, the arrival of the Magi; the *Ecce Homo* and the throng of sinister faces, the "hydra", the sarcasms in the Ghent *Christ Carrying the Cross*, the sadistic joy of the torturers: all that happens when a crowd is unrestrained. In his works there are punishments, tortures, the Deadly Sins, Hell, the martyrdom of Saint Julia, the Crucifixion, the Temptations and the "waning of the Middle Ages", according to Huizinga's thesis: in essence, a crossroads, with a background of gnostic and alchemical elements. There is flight, the flying ship and "levitation" (a fact which is never mentioned), anticlerical satire; fools (*The Ship of Fools*); the fall of the rebel angels; the sacrifice of Noah shown on Melchior's collar (Prado *Adoration*); peasant dances (left panel of the Prado *Adoration*; *Prodigal Son*); hybrids raining from heaven, or liberating themselves into space. Is this a licence allowed to nature, while a much more significant event is taking place?

Especially in the *Temptations* the allegorical figures shaped like birds or fish or flying boats, all forms taken by the hybrids, permit a very useful examination of the dreams and acts of androgyne sexuality.

The relationship between the event and the object (*Epiphany*, *Magi* and other characters present, very strange and rich in meaning) constitute the "expressions" depicted by a work of art. They are relationships implying the idea (characteristic of imaginative art) and the presentation of objects (in the *Epiphany*) shown as forms. In a period of indirect controversy it is an attempt to show, for example under cover of exoticism, the coming of the Magi and the presentation of homage, coming from a different world. It is a hidden exoticism, in a way, but it shows the richness of the sources, thanks to the insertion into the picture of very disturbing "additional evidence". Bosch is the historiographer of all foreign sources, which converge in an apparently hagiographical scene. What is hidden behind the primary meaning is of fundamental importance.

There are other events—always involving protest and a multiplicity of meanings: disguises (masks, costumes, Carnival, hybrids); Sabbats (Lisbon *Temptations*) and enigmatic "flights" which are not a fruit of the imagination: they mean the unexpected assembly to which the hermit is brought, having already had to face the gathering of the hybrids, "significant" meetings of monsters in space and on the waters.

There is the banquet, the "sacrifice" of the swan (Lisbon *Temptations*) and the L-shaped table of the heretics; pleasures, in the *Earthly Paradise* of the Doge's Palace, contemplation, visions (the picture of *St John on Patmos* and the *Temptations*)—under the influence of hallucinogens or as a result of asceticism? Noise and shouts are an unexpected accompaniment; these non-conceptual paintings are full of uproar.

We also understand by events the lesson of facts and the reflection of the period, the fruit of a life "full of struggles", and certain psychopathological phenomena which can be reconstructed, beginning with "St Anthony's fire", the metal bar with a ring, beside the magus (in the Lisbon *Temptation* and that of Brussels, besides a tapestry copied from Bosch, exhibited at Bordeaux in 1968, and undoubtedly woven at Brussels about 1556, catalogue no. 5).

Finally we must not forget the "journey" of the Pilgrim or the Fool, Prodigal and Sage, and the meetings resulting from it. On the other hand every brotherhood received visitors of importance, initiates. Who? It seems that Bosch was at a crossroads, at the confluence of traditions which we do not know, but which undoubtedly emerge here and there in themes which we have constantly recorded and defined in the course of this study.

If we think about the period, many reflections of it appear in Bosch's works, often shot through with a fine exoticism: *Magi*, including the "black king", Caspar (*Epiphany*, Prado), one of the most splendid figures of his bizarre repertoire; the *elephant* of A. de Hameel, then of J. Cock (35).

The theme of the *wild man* is certainly the cue for a "procession", but a secular one, worthy of the festivities on the occasion of the entry of personalities, including civil liturgies. Finally we cannot underestimate the function of the Mystery plays, since Bosch was the inventor and constructor of machines, masks and costumes.

Bosch, passionately interested in Hebraism, does not admit any prohibition and takes from every source (before the advent of the book).

Experiences, phenomena and sources inspire fear or attraction, which suggests the presence of a "force" of which the seat is unknown. In the body or the mind? In a mysterious "beyond" which would become accessible through rites and practices? But which?

These events must first be traced in the work. Julian Huxley suggests that we can distinguish three different kinds: external (volcanic eruptions, lightning), biological (disease, death), psychological (obsession, visions, madness).

This general order is considered sacred or rather, according to R. Caillois, "it constitutes sacredness". Prohibition and taboo have no other purpose than to ensure its preservation, but to

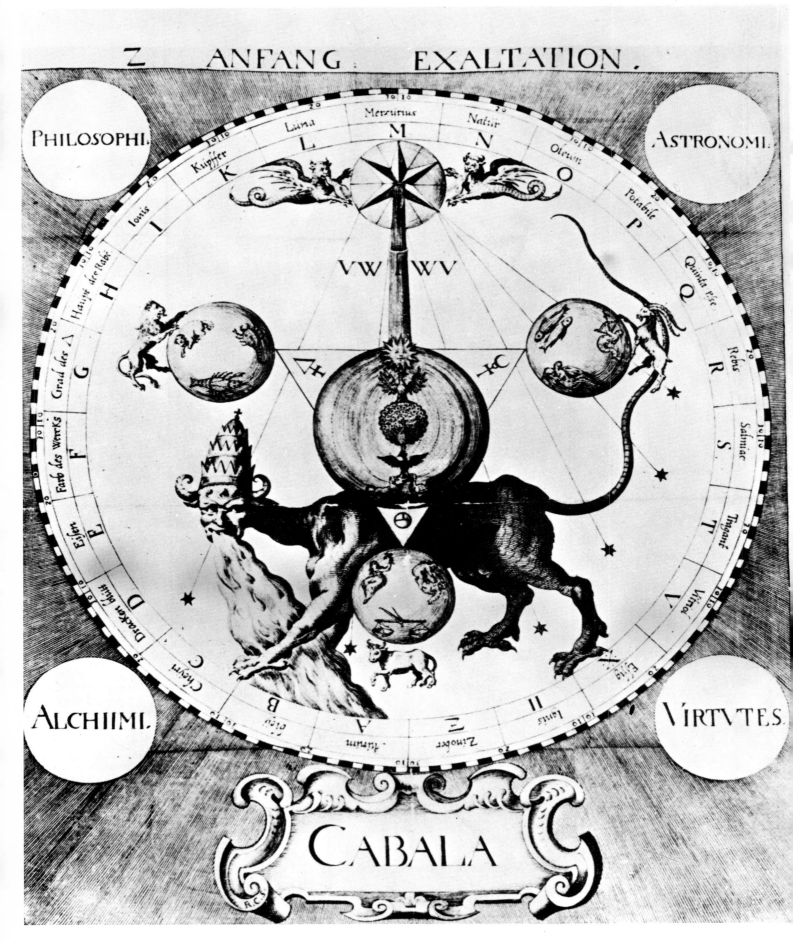

transgress means to go beyond. Where? Towards magic, dangerous rites, familiarity with the emblematic figures known to Bosch, as the strange symbolism shows. Ceremonies, sacrifices, expiations "serve only to re-integrate this sacredness".

The biological or psychopathological phenomena pointed out by Huxley as "the principal supports of the religious sentiment cease to be so"; it is possible to explain them and thus deconsecrate them "without religion suffering. It finds other means of support".

Bosch's imagination incessantly evokes and puts into his work feasts and ceremonies celebrated in the sanctuary (importance of the altar in *The Marriage at Cana*) in the presence of the faithful, of a brotherhood or group: that of the founders and the initiates. Cryptic art is full of such relationships.

HEAVEN

A heaven impossible to imagine, that of astral mythology and mysterious rites (astrology and hermetic science are among Bosch's sources) might with its presence and after being so frequently invoked, make one forget the celestial sweetness. It is a curious euphemism when we think of the terrible universe of imaginative art, and the past with its cruelty and tortures. To compile a list of faults, they said, is nothing; all that counts is the glory of God.

It is certain that this affirmation is continually attacked by Bosch who, according to the iconographic laws in use, shows the Heavenly Father in the empyrean, if the vault is really the image of heaven, at least from the architectural point of view.

On another plane, a study should be made of the light and the spectacle of heaven, which seems to worry nordic man (like Dürer in *Melancholy*). Taking into account a certain theology, perhaps Alexandrine, or the agnosticism inherent in the "clandestine activity of a sect", in Bosch heaven is a metaphysical chaos, origin and home of the hybrids, after the fall, and where we become lost. The ineffable delights are reserved for the Elect, and their ascent into the Empyrean is saluted with a hymn of glory.

According to astrology, taught in the schools, and very widespread in Bosch's time, Helios is the lord of heaven; as for the divisions in accordance with the Tables of the Decans, it is well known that, from the time of the Egyptians, the sun-god was linked with the decans. All hermetic science converges in Bosch's work.

The heavens deified obviously imply a god of the heavens, or rather of the classical divinities. Bosch excels in the clandestine war against militant hagiography: the rediscovery of earlier myths, from before the revelation of dogma. Hence the importance of the celestial vault and the orb, the keystone which allows the tide of hybrids to break out and spread, a vast swarm "on which other phenomena take place". In the Middle Ages the idea of nature was very complex; the sky is also a source of observations (36); the path of the sun, moon and stars, storms, the rainbow which, in the west, is a warning.

In mythology, there is a certain hieratic order, even based on the earthly one: the "god of heaven" in his glory has rather a baroque air of royalty and occupies the first and highest rank. It is a strange hierarchy which includes the flying angels, creatures of celestial grace, azure and rose. For Bosch, the anthropomorphism of heaven is certainly only a pretext: further down, below the line of the horizon, fire is consuming the towers, shattered and crumbling.

's-HERTOGENBOSCH

Now the chief town of the province of North Brabant, Bosch's city owes its fame to Duke Henry I of Brabant, who gave it civic rights in 1185. In the fourteenth and fifteenth centuries it enjoyed a period of great prosperity; famous for fairs, knives and its school (where Erasmus studied) it was one of the most important towns in Brabant.

In 1481 Emperor Maximilian I held there, in the choir of the cathedral, the fourteenth general assembly of the chapter of the Golden Fleece. Outside, the cathedral has some curious details, including the statuetted placed astride the rampant arches.

In the city is the headquarters of the Brotherhood of Our Lady founded in 1318.

The city developed under Philip the Good, Duke of Burgundy, the great Duke of the West, patron of the arts. The great fire of 1463 must certainly have impressed young Bosch, as must also the riots, sackings and wars that struck it from 1470 to 1477.

In 1482 the Burgundian dynasty died out. In 1504 Duke Philip the Handsome visited Bosch's workshop and commissioned a Last Judgment.

The authorities of 's-Hertogenbosch enjoyed a great reputation, and the ceremonies, processions and festivals of the city were famous. The function of the brotherhoods and the schools of rhetoric forms an important chapter in the history of sects and associations.

THE NUDE

The nude is rather rare in Bosch's time, and we cannot help admiring his alchemical beauties: the woman in front of the hollow tree, and the nudes of the *Temptations* and *The Garden of Delights*, not to mention the appearance of a few black ones, without any mannered exoticism. Generally Eve is very licentious, more so than the characters of the *Allegory of Pleasures* (18). Boys, or the baby with the windmill in *Christ Carrying the Cross* (19) have an attractive grace.

The importance of a few details is often forgotten: the partial nakedness of initiation: the right shoulder in the Escorial *Christ Crowned with Thorns*, and the right knee in *The Prodigal Son*. In such cases the figure can lead to the discovery of arcane meanings.

We have already admired his peculiarity of showing the figure from behind (women with beautiful buttocks, the damned with a sword run through the anus, the disturbing *Tree-man*, *The Alchemical Man*) or even a certain tendency to elongate them; as in *The Garden of Delights*. But there are also contracted figures (heads with legs, head alone) squatting with scatological intent or with their limbs fragmented (20). Signs and symbols are proper to the period; the oyster is the female genitals and the knife the male, while St Jerome symbolises the wise man.

In the study of characters and types the problem is one of passing from the physiological to the psychological plane, without neglecting the importance of gestures or of the hieratic.

Sometimes an obese character, with a swollen belly, appears in a scene, as on the head of the *Tree-man*, next to the bagpipes. Perhaps it is the image of a drunkard, but it is not clear why it accompanies the naked pederast.

The altercation between the loser and the winner bursts into violence, and the knife is thrust into the back of the man who has won. In this scene there is always a certain insensibility to blows, and the two men continue to talk to each other.

Gesticulation is revealing but hermetic, and it would be necessary to carry out a study, beginning with the movements of the fingers, of the manner of indicating or taking, like the wand of the magus in *The Marriage at Cana*.

There is a language of the fingers, which has become enigmatic for us, but which was taught in the lodges. We think of the importance of the hand as an amulet, or perhaps a severed foot, adopted as a relic. Other gestures are more easily recognisable, such as that of benediction.

Bosch's fantastic art takes account of details: eyes, ears, hands and the gesture of grasping or blessing, taking or attacking, breaking or torturing. In virtue of the capacity for expression, the care devoted to every detail, a special power is transmitted to the eyes and at the same time to the ears; to the eyes with the marvels of prodigious fantasy, the proliferation of hybrids of disconcerting agility, with a frightening strength like that of the armed body that becomes a cart; with the image and life of shapes, the swarm of which seems to depend on the magician *Hermogenes* (Valenciennes Museum) or Satan; to the ears with proverbs and sayings, the function of which in Bosch's work is known, with saws and maxims, the stuff of secrecy, fragments to be deciphered and understood.

The whole being of the future observer is involved in this art of the augur and the oracle, which "reads" in the shape of the body.

In the realm of hybrid and contracted beings, we are struck by the importance of asymmetric details: certain organs in the embryonic state, with origins in fable. The unexpected cessation of growth, stumps or mutilation would mean the deviation caused by over-development; but, in compensation, the hybrids proliferate, menacing or frightening the hermit.

A tempter-figure, the nude illustrates the fascination of the naked body, of the wide-legged attitude, the gleam of flesh. But in hell the tortures of the stake or the spit predominate over the activities of naked couples, as a reminder of the punishments awaiting those who commit the sins of the flesh.

Bosch's monsters were perhaps inspired by the acrobats and jugglers who were much in evidence in the Middle Ages. M. Picard believes that acrobats did not perform simply to entertain, but that they re-enacted ancient rites. Thus from the strange acrobatics among Bosch's hybrids we could also learn something of the licentious life of the fairs in his time. They must undoubtedly have recalled Alcuin's precept: "Whoever introduces into his house actors, mimes and dancers does not realise that he is letting in a legion of devils with their train". But Bosch gives a prominent place to actors and acrobats, not to mention beggars.

This way of understanding the body should be more widespread; too many restrictions are wrong. Man should have complete familiarity with his own body and with the discovery through love (and not as a voyeur) of another body. What, then, is it about the bodies and nudes of Bosch, of the monsters and hybrids which arouse a wonder that is always new?

The hybrid, being unnatural, arouses our curiosity; from the hybrid to the monster, through the nudes, Bosch has been able to exploit the whole range, and to interest us with certain hairy figures which make us think, not of the Satanic type, but of the wild man, endowed with impressive power when he gives proof of his strength and violence.

Bosch grafts on to his reality a lively festival of strangeness that even today has all the qualities to seduce us. Behind the fables, behind the bizarre shapes, is truth. From this comes a way, all Bosch's own, of covering the entire physical and psychical field through the resources of art. But in virtue of the many signs and symbols, not to mention the new values which the hybrid brings with it, imaginative art remains in part mysterious.

Thus the statement is something like this: with and through my body I am in the real world and in the world of monsters, and as a result of this multiform content, in the cosmos.

The first statement proclaims the limits of the finite, largely exploited by religious art. The second, ignored until then, introduces us to a gnosis, where we need to compile a collection of the notions and concepts characteristic of imaginative art, as far from conventional allegorical interpretation as if we were always in unexplored territory. It is perhaps a curious virgin territory—a forbidden zone—with the body as mediator: even before being the oyster-shell (of which Plato speaks) and the Tomb of the Orphists, it is an opening. Thanks to Bosch's imaginative art, the body receives experiences and expresses ideas, and to receive is a way of being open to the world.

As a sign to others, according to Ricoeur (21) my body "makes me mysterious" (and the same is true of other people's bodies) and open to "the mutual exchange of consciousness".

SHEPHERDS

The shepherds of the *Epiphany* are very ambiguous characters, who do not pay much attention to the sacred scene. Is it the unselfconsciousness of people incapable of understanding the event, or indifference, the hostility of the layman or peasant towards anything that could disturb his world?

On the thatched roof of the stable (Prado *Epiphany*) we see nomads dressed in the colours of the plain, according to Tolnay (37). The "profane world" wants to see with its own eyes; the roof, which is coming to pieces above the divine group, acts as a divider.

These rascally shepherds, rogues or vagabonds, have a disturbing air, as equivocal as the cripples.

(1) Cf. Paracelso, 1493–1541: Agrippa, 1486–1535.
(2) Cf. Seligman, p. 103.
(3) Groddeck, p. 86.
(4) Enrico Castelli, *Le démoniaque dans l'art*, p. 115.
(5) Jacques Lacan, *Ecrits*, pp. 97–98.
(6) Lucien Febvre, *Le probleme de l'incroyance au XVI siecle*, pp. 17–18
(7) Lucien Febvre, op. cit., p. 18.
(8) Lucien Febvre, op. cit., p. 154.
(9) Anthony Bosman, p. 5.
(10) Guidici, IV, 4.
(11) Boehme, *Mysterium Magnum*, cf. XXIV, XVI.
(12) P. 145.
(13) Cf. *Alcibiade premier*, p. 107.
(14) P. 32.
(15) Origene, p. 47.
(16) Aepli, *Reve*, p. 33.
(17) Kerenyi, *Fripon divin*, p. 168.
(18) Mia Cinotti, p. 17.
(19) Mia Cinotti, p. 19.
(20) Cf. Lacan, *Ecrits*.
(21) P. Ricoer, *Dialectique*, ed. Desclee, *Negativite et affirmation*, p. 103.
(22) Charles Tolnay, p. 25.
(23) Jacques Lacan, p. VII.
(24) Enrico Castelli, p. 116.
(25) Anthony Bosman, p. 73.
(26) Uekkull, *Mondeis animaux*, p. 36.
(27) Jean Gessler in Misc., LV Puyvelde, p. 271.
(28) Robert Mandrou, *Introduction à la France Moderne*, p. 34.
(29) J. Huizinga, *Le declin du Moyen Age*, p. 209.
(30) J. Huizinga, *Le declin du Moyen Age*, p. 29.
(31) W. Deonna, *Le symbolisme de l'acrobatie antique*, 1953, p. 126.
(32) Robert Graves, *Myths*, p. 53.
(33) René Guenon, *Symboles fondamentaux de la science sacrée* 1962 p. 75.
(34) Wilhelm Fraenger, p. 18.
(35) Mia Cinotti, p. 117.
(36) Norman Cohn, *Les fanatiques de l'Apocalypse*, p. 145.
(37) Tolnay, p. 44.

1450	Birth of Jeroen or Joen van Aaken (Aeken, Acken) at 's-Hertogenbosch, in North Brabant. J. Mosmans suggests as the birth-date October 2nd, 1453. Den Bosch is the usual abbreviation of the name of the town. It was fairly common to derive a name from the place of origin and the patron saint, giving the signature: HIERONYMUS (Jheronimus) BOSCH.
1450	Gutenberg opened a printing shop at Magonza. *Last Judgment* of R. Van der Weyden.
1453	Crowning of the Virgin of Enguerrant Quarton at Villeneuve-les-Avignon.
1455-56	Death of Bosch's grandfather Van Aken, painter of frescoes mentioned in 1444. Bosch's education is still obscure.
1457	Quarrel between Nicholas of Cues and Sigismund of Austria over the reform of the secular clergy.
1459	The Strasbourg Lodge, according to H. Haug (1) was from 1459 the supreme lodge among all those of the cathedrals of the Holy Roman Empire.
1460	The first international stock exchange was opened at Antwerp.
1461-1534	Campanile of St Bavo at Ghent.
1462	Triptych of the Magi by van der Weyden.
1464-68	Polyptych of the Last Supper by Thierry Bouts.
1467	Philip the Good succeeded by Charles the Bold, who dreamed of uniting the Netherlands with Burgundy.
1468	Sacking of Ghent and first tortures in the public squares of the Netherlands "to combat the action of the devil". The paintings of Bosch show the tortures used by the Inquisition Using religious subjects as a cover, he shows the period with its scenes of violence in a most unfavourable light. The performance of medieval Mystery plays often inflamed the crowd with anti-semitism, and the ghettos had to be guarded by armed men.

1468	Charles the Bold conquered Liège.
1470	Guillaume Fichet introduced the art of printing to the Sorbonne.
1471-1528	Life of Albrecht Dürer.
1473-1542	Life of Copernicus.
1474	Alsace rose against the Burgundians; rebellion of Cologne.
1475	Death at Zwolle of Alain de la Roche, a Dominican monk. In his sermons he used a strange bestiary of animals to symbolise sin These may have been a source of Bosch's bestiary.
1475	Foundation of the University of Upsala.
1477	Marriage of Marie of Burgundy with Prince Maximilian of Austria.
1477	Maximilian of Austria again took up the struggle against the republican cities.
1478	A Dutch translation of the *Golden Legend* of Jacobus de Voragine one of the sources of the *Temptations St Anthony* was printed at Gouda.
1478	Louis XI prohibited the activities of the Inquisition in the Melusine Alps of Jean d'Arras.
1478-94	Alaert (Allaert) du (de) Hameel, architect and engraver, in charge of the building of the cathedral of St John at 's-Hertogenbosch, finished the south wing of the transept and began the central nave. The importance of the Lodges, which flourished under the protection of the cathedrals, is well known. The grotesque figures adorning the rampant arches of the choir are one of the probable sources of the fantastic element in Bosch's work.

1480	As an engraver, A. du Hameel became the interpreter of Bosch's work.
1480-81	Bosch is mentioned for the first time as being married. He was reasonably well-off, which helps to explain the artist's intellectual independence.
1480-81	Bosch acquired two panels of the altarpiece for the Brotherhood of Our Lady at 's-Hertogenbosch, which his father had left unfinished (Mosmans, Mc, 84). Bosch was described as *Jeroen de maeire* (Jerome the painter).
1481	Institution of the Inquisition in Spain—Torquemada.
1482	Publication of the Dutch version *Het boek van Tondalus vysioen* (*Visio Tundali*), the work of an Irishman. Tundal, who lived in the 12th century, visited in spirit the land beyond the grave, and three days later returned to his own body. It is a dark vision, which represents one of the sources of "visionary" iconography.
1482	Bosch inherited a small property at Roedeken, near Oerschot.
1484	On December 5th the Papal Bull *Summis desiderantes affectibus* was published, denouncing magicians and heretics and beginning the great persecution, an echo of which is found in Bosch's work. A triumph of exoticism: an elephant was exhibited at 's-Hertogenbosch (2). Erasmus, at the age of seventeen, went to 's-Hertogenbosch and spent some not very happy years with the Brothers of the Free Spirit which he considered wasted. We have not seen the end of the long discussions on the affiliations of Bosch (and Dürer) to this or that sect, and on the nature of the "occult culture" of that period. There are undeniably various trends, which can only be described as forerunners of the Rosicrucians. Without paying too much attention to the history of the sects, since documentary evidence is lacking, *The Marriage at Cana* reveals the existence of a sect. But which? However, Bosch's interest in Jewish questions and problems, including exegesis, is obvious. To trace the various subterranean currents is a difficult undertaking which may be clarified by the study of symbols.

1484	Self-portrait of Dürer (silver-point).
1486	Dürer apprenticed to Michael Wohlgemut.
1486-87	Bosch joined the Brotherhood of Our Lady (*Lieve Vrouwe Broederschap*) of the Cathedral of St John at 's-Hertogenbosch, founded in 1318. We know the importance of these institutions in organising Mysteries and processions, with a liturgy that was not necessarily orthodox, outside the places reserved for the official cult. The brotherhood had as its emblem a swan (not to be confused with the sign of some inns considered to be "questionable places") and every year a "banquet of the swan" was celebrated.
1487	The inquisitor Henricus Kramer published at Strasbourg the *Malleus Maleficarum*, the Hammer of Witches, for the use of inquisitors, in which the practices of wizards were described, and repression became fierce. In certain aspects, Bosch's work is an anthology of these practices and a history of tortures. It can thus be seen as a denunciation of the Inquisition.
1488	Bosch figured as a "notable" of the group of members of the Brotherhood of Our Lady and presided at the annual banquet. He is repeatedly mentioned in the archives of the brotherhood: 1489, 1493, 1498, 1503. According to Ebeling, Bosch became a master in 1487/88. The engraver Alaert du Hameel was also a member of the brotherhood.
1488	Crusade against the Waldenses. Maximilian transferred to Antwerp the commercial privileges of Bruges. Triptych of the Frari by Giovanni Bellini.
1489-92	Bosch painted the panels of the picture on the high altar of the Brotherhood of Our Lady. This work is now lost; it showed Abigail and David.
1490	A translation of the lives of the saints, *Vitae patrum*, taken from Saint Anastasius and including a life of St Anthony, was published at Zwolle.
1490	Marriage of Anne of Brittany and Maximilian of Austria.

1490-94	Dürer's visit to Colmar and Basle.
1492	Bosch prepared the design for a stained glass window to be placed in the chapel of the brotherhood.
1492	Expulsion of the Jews from Spain.
1493	Era of Florentine Mannerism.
1494	*The Ship of Fools* (*Das Narrenschiff*) of Sebastian Brant was printed at Basle. It was translated into French in 1497.
1494	*Ars Moralis* of Lefèvre d'Etaples.
1494-1553	Aldo Manuzio founded his printing shop in Venice.
1496	The baptism of the Jew Jacob de Almaengien took place at 's-Hertogenbosch in the presence of Philip the Handsome; according to Fraenger he was the Grand Master of the Free Spirit. It is possible that some of the strange symbolism in *The Marriage at Cana* was inspired by him. Subsequently Almaengien returned to Judaism.
1496	Forced conversion of the Jews and Moors in Portugal.
1497	Marriage of Marguerite de Bourgogne with Don Juan.
1498	Excommunication of Gerolamo Savonarola.
1498	Henry VII brought the trade in woollen materials back to Antwerp. Dürer's *Apocalypse*.
1500	Lyons became a second capital and residence of the court. *Adagia* of Erasmus. Convention of the Order of St John of Jerusalem at Belem.

1503-04	It appears from the account-books of the Brotherhood of Our Lady that Bosch received a commission to paint three shields.
1504	It appears from a document in the Lille archives (no. F.190) that Bosch received thirty-six lire in payment for a picture ordered by Philip the Handsome which was to present the Last Judgment with Paradise and Hell. This work may be the Vienna *Last Judgment* or the fragmentary one at Munich.
1506	*Ruidmenta linguae hebraicae* by Reuchlin. *La Gioconda* of Leonardo.
1508-09	The priors of the Brotherhood of Our Lady asked advice from Bosch and from the architect of their chapel, Jean Heynste or Heyns, about the polychroming and gilding of a carved altarpiece.
1508-12	The brotherhood paid the painter for "the design of a candelabrum" in copper.
1510	Isenheim altarpiece by Matthias Grünewald.
1511	*Praise of Folly* by Erasmus. *Augenspiegel* by Reuchlin.
1511-12	Bosch designed "a cross or a cruxifix" perhaps for a cotta, commissioned by his brotherhood (5).
1513	Reuchlin condemned by the Inquisition.
1515	*St Jerome* by Erasmus.
1516	In the inventory of the possessions at Malines of Margaret of Austria, sister of Philip the Handsome, Regent of the Netherlands, there is listed a *St Anthony* painted by Bosch. 9th August: The funeral of Bosch, *insignis pictor* (a distinguished painter), took place in the chapel of the Brotherhood.
1516	*Orlando Furioso* by Ariosto. *Utopia* by Thomas More. *Edition of the New Testament* by Erasmus.
1520	Don Felipe de Guevara inherited from his father an art collection, including works by Bosch, which was at Brussels.

1521	M. A. Michiel saw three pictures by Bosch in Venice, at the home of Cardinal Grimani.
1523-24	Damião de Gois, agent of John III, bought a picture by Bosch inspired by the patience of Job.
1531	Inventory of the goods left by Aleyt van de Meervenne, Bosch's widow.
1535	Guevara transported his collection, including some pictures by Bosch, to Madrid.
1560-62	Guevara wrote the *Comentarios de la pintura*, in which he speaks of Bosch. "Recently I found another kind of picture called 'grillo' or caprice. It is an amusing type, mentioned by Pliny, and made fashionable by Antiphilus, about 500 B.C.". It is known that in Greek "grillo" means pig, and that a companion of Ulysses of this name refused to be changed back into a man after being turned into a pig.
1570	Philip II of Spain acquired various works by Bosch: *The Haywain, Three Blind Men, Flemish Dance, Blind Men, Witch, Cure for Folly*.
1574	Philip II, having gained possession of other works by Bosch, had nine of his pictures transported to the Escorial (6), and had *The Seven Deadly Sins* hung in his room. Other works, which remained in the Royal Palace, were mainly lost.
1586	Ambrosio de Morales describes *The Haywain* in his commentary on the *Tabla de Cebes*; this text may date from earlier than 1570. Morales had known Guevara's collection since 1544–45.

(1) He was the curator of the Museum of the Works of Our Lady, created in 1931 near the cathedral in Strasbourg. It was perhaps linked with the Brotherhood of Our Lady in Bosch's time. Mithart spent his years of apprenticeship in Flanders and then in the Rhineland after 1475 and before 1479. Dürer's travels give some information on the "tour" of apprenticeship. Bosch was admitted as master and initiated, but after what "journeys"?
(2) Mia Cinotti, p. 117.
(3) Cf. M. Ghyka, II Rites, p. 79, no. 4.
(4) Cf. *The Ship of Fools*, Paris, Louvre.
(5) Mia Cinotti, p. 85.
(6) Mia Cinotti, p. 85.

Bibliography

A selected list of general works; an exhaustive bibliography can be found in Delevoy's book (1960) and in Tolnay's 1965 edition.

F. de Guevara	*Commentarios de la pintura (1560–62)* Madrid—1788
C. van Mander	*Het Schilderboeck* Haarlem—1604 (trans. English by C. van de Wall, *Dutch and Flemish Painters* New York—1936)
J. de Sigüença	*Tercera parte de la Historia de la Orden de S. Gerónimo* Madrid—1605
J. B. Gramaye	*Taxandria* Brussels—1610
A. Ponz	*Viaje de España* Madrid—1772–94
A. Pinchart	*Documents inédits, I* in "Archives des Arts, Sciences et Lettres"—Gand—1860
M. Viñaza	*Adiciones al Diccionario de Ceãn Bermudez* Madrid—1889
C. Justi	*Hieronymus Bosch, 1889* Berlin—1908
M. G. Gossart	*Jérôme Bosch, "Le faizeur de diables"* Lille—1907
L. Maeterlinck	*Le genre satirique dans la peinture flamande* Brussels—1907
P. Lafond	*Hieronymus Bosch* Brussels—1914
M. J. Friedländer	*Von Eyck bis Bruegel* Berlin—1916 & 1921
M. Dvorak	*Kunstgeshichte als Geissesgeschichte* Monaco—1921
M. J. Friedländer	*Geerten und Bosch* Berlin—1927
D. Hannema & J. G. van Gelder	*Catalogue de l'Exposition: Jeroen Bosch* Rotterdam—1936
A. M. Hammacher	*Jeroen Bosch* Vreije Bladen—1936
Ch. de Tolnay	*Hieronymus Bosch* Basle—1937 & Baden Baden—1965
W. Ganzenmuller	*L'alchimie au Moyen Age* Paris—1940
M. J. Friedländer	*Bosch* La Haye—1941

L. Baldass	*Hieronymus Bosch* Vienna—1941 & 1950
L. Van de Bossche	*Jérôme Bosch* Diest—1944
J. Combe	*Jérôme Bosch* Paris—1946 & 1957
J. De Bosschère	*Jérôme Bosch* Brussels—1947
D. Bax	*Ontcijfering van Jeroen Bosch* La Haye—1949
J. Leymarie	*Bosch* Paris—1949
G. Welter	*Histoire des sectes chrétiennes* Paris—1950
W. Fraenger	*Die Hochzeit zu Kana, Ein Document semitische Gnosis bei H. B.* Berlin—1950
W. Fraenger	*Der Tisch der Weisheit bisher "Die sieben Todsünden" genannt* Stockholm—1951
W. Fraenger	*The Millennium of Hieronymus Bosch, Outlines of a new interpretation* London—1952
E. Castelli	*Il Demoniaco nell'arte* Milan—1952
E. Panofsky	*Early Netherlandish Painting* Cambridge, Mass.—1953
L. Brandt-Philip	*The Prado Epiphany by Jérôme Bosch* in "The Art Bulletin"—1953—n. 35
L. Van Puyvelde	*Les primitifs flamands* Brussels—1954
J. Baltrusaitis	*Le Moyen Age fantastique* Paris—1955
G. Dorfles	*Bosch* Milan—1954
M. Brion	*Bosch, Goya et le fantastique* Bordeaux—1957

E. Fulcanelli — *Le mystère des cathédrales*
Paris—1957

J. Lassaigne — *La peinture flamande au siècle de Bosch e Brueghel*
Geneva—1957

A. Wertheim-Aymès — *Hieronymus Bosch*
Amsterdam—1957

W. Hirsck — *Hieronymus Bosch and the Thinking of the Late Middle Ages*
Stockholm—1957

R. Salvini — *La pittura fiamminga*
Milan—1958

G. Linfert — *Hieronymus Bosch*
London—1959

R. H. Wilensky — *Flemish Painters*
London—1960

R. L. Delevoy — *Bosch*
Geneva—1960

C. Roy — *Les arts fantastiques*
Paris—1960

L. Van Puyvelde — *La peinture flamande au siècle de Bosch et Breughel*
Paris—1962

M. Gauffreteau-Sévy — *Jérôme Bosch*
Paris—1965

M. Cinotti—D. Buzzati — *Bosch*
Milan—1966

M. Bussagli — *Bosch*
Florence—1966